INTRODUCING

Aesthetics

Christopher Kul-Want • Piero

Icon Books UK   Totem Books USA

Published in the UK
in 2007 by Icon Books Ltd.,
The Old Dairy, Brook Road,
Thriplow, Cambridge SG8 7RG
email: info@iconbooks.co.uk
www.introducingbooks.com

Sold in the UK, Europe, South Africa
and Asia by Faber and Faber Ltd.,
3 Queen Square, London WC1N 3AU
or their agents

Distributed in the UK, Europe, South
Africa and Asia by TBS Ltd., TBS
Distribution Centre, Colchester Road,
Frating Green, Colchester CO7 7DW

Published in Australia
in 2007 by Allen & Unwin Pty. Ltd.,
PO Box 8500, 83 Alexander Street,
Crows Nest, NSW 2065

Published in the USA
in 2007 by Totem Books
Inquiries to Icon Books Ltd.,
The Old Dairy, Brook Road,
Thriplow, Cambridge
SG8 7RG, UK

Distributed to the trade in the USA by
National Book Network Inc.,
4501 Forbes Boulevard, Suite 200
Lanham, Maryland 20706

Distributed in Canada by
Penguin Books Canada,
90 Eglinton Avenue East, Suite 700,
Toronto, Ontario M4P 2YE

ISBN-10: 1-84046-790-8
ISBN-13: 978-1840467-90-1

Printed and bound in Singapore
by Tien Wah Press

John Keats

So the Romantic poet **John Keats** (1795–1821) wrote in his celebrated meditation upon mortality and immortality, "Ode on a Grecian Urn" of 1820. But what is beauty, and what is truth? These are some of the questions which aesthetics tries to answer.

What is Aesthetics?

Aesthetics (the plural form of aesthetic) is derived from the Greek word *aisthētikos*, from *aisthēta*, meaning things perceptible by the senses. In the 18th century aesthetics became a branch of philosophy. The German philosopher **Alexander Gottlieb Baumgarten** (1714–62) first used the word in his *Reflections on Certain Matters Relating to Poetry* of 1735. Then, in 1750, Baumgarten entitled an unfinished treatise *Aesthetica*.

AESTHETICS IS A SPECIALIST AREA OF INQUIRY CONCERNED WITH PERCEPTION AND SENSORY EXPERIENCE.

Today, the word "aesthetic" is frequently encountered in its negative form: "anaesthetic", which refers to a substance that induces an absence of sensation and an inability to feel pain.

Aesthetics has come to be used not just in relation to philosophy, but also in connection with design and fashion (e.g. the designer of a car will refer to its aesthetics, or an interior designer will use the word to refer to the look and style of their designs). In a similar way, "aesthetic" is used in connection with art to describe the sensibility and style of an artist's work.

Having the same root as aesthetic, the word "aesthete" refers to a person who professes a superior appreciation of what is beautiful. Oscar Wilde, who dedicated his life and work to a love of art and beauty, is often cited as an aesthete. Wilde believed that art should be valued for itself alone and not for any purpose or function.

THE ONLY EXCUSE FOR MAKING SOMETHING USELESS IS THAT ONE ADMIRES IT INTENSELY.

ALL ART IS USELESS.

Wilde attempted to preserve an area of aesthetic experience – the appreciation of beauty – apart from utilitarian values fostered by Capitalist economics. The tradition of *philosophical* aesthetics on the Continent went further than Wilde by questioning whether experience could be represented or assigned a moral value. This tradition had its origins in the 18th century.

The Nature of Experience

Following Baumgarten, aesthetics as a philosophical activity became concerned not just with the question of beauty but with the whole **nature of experience** in terms of perceptions, feelings and emotions. Philosophers, however, quickly realized that this inquiry opened out onto issues of subjectivity and identity and the potential for transforming values and beliefs. This is because the issue of experience relates to the question of consciousness and, by implication, the role of unconscious experience in shaping identity. So, while aesthetics began as a specialist branch of philosophy, it was actually in the right position to form the kernel for nearly all future philosophical inquiry.

THE SUBJECT OF EXPERIENCE BECAME BOUND UP WITH QUESTIONS OF POLITICS, PSYCHOANALYSIS AND ART ---

--- AND, MORE WIDELY, WITH THE VITAL ISSUES OF MODERNITY AND POSTMODERNITY.

Prior to Baumgarten, aesthetics did not exist in name as such. Nevertheless, there existed a long-standing and important tradition in philosophy which was concerned with the meaning and significance of perception and sensory experience. This tradition stretches back to Plato and classical philosophy, in which issues of beauty and truth were first coupled together.

Socrates and Plato

It is important to bear in mind that, in the classical period, truth was associated with religious and ethical ideas. Plato's philosophy was based on the teachings of his mentor, the itinerant philosopher **Socrates** (470–399 BC). In common with the rest of Greek society, Socrates held religious beliefs which were **metaphysical** in character. Metaphysics is a *dualistic* system – the gods exist in a higher transcendent realm and the world down below, inhabited by humans, is a pale imitation of it.

THERE EXISTS AN UNDERLYING, TRANSCENDENT ORDER TO THE UNIVERSE.

THIS ORDER IS COMPOSED OF ETERNALLY EXISTING FORMS FROM WHICH WE DERIVE ABSOLUTE VALUES OF JUSTICE, BEAUTY AND TRUTH.

In addition, Socrates stated that these Forms contained the inherent structures to be found within all existing objects. However, he differed from the majority of Greek society by valuing wisdom and virtue in contrast to the warrior's attributes of bravery and strength, which were thought to find favour with the gods.

8

Following Socrates, **Plato** (c. 427–347 BC) argued that philosophers, such as himself, were uniquely in possession of the correct virtue – namely, wisdom – for attaining knowledge of the higher Forms of the universe. By defying currently held views, Socrates and Plato embarked on a power struggle with the state and religious hierarchy of Athens. As a way of defining his position, Plato contrasted philosophy with both art and poetry, which he stated were immoral and untruthful.

ART AND POETRY ARE "MIMETIC", IN OTHER WORDS, MERELY IMITATIVE.

THEY PLAY UPON PEOPLE'S EMOTIONS.

On account of their dangerous influence, Plato in *The Republic* (c. 375 BC) banned artists and poets from his ideal state.

The Power of Poetry

The idea of poetry's power to affect the viewer was a loaded issue in Plato's time. Poets were believed to have access to the muses, the daughters of memory who possessed historical knowledge and insight into the gods' motives. Furthermore, poetry had a high public profile since plays were written in verse; it was also the custom to read poetry aloud in public forums.

I DISAPPROVE OF THE POWER OF POETRY TO SEDUCE PEOPLE.

IT GIVES A FALSE VIEW OF THE GODS AND PROVIDES UNSUITABLE MODELS OF BEHAVIOUR TO THE YOUNG AND IMPRESSIONABLE.

In making his negative judgement of poetry, Plato particularly castigated the work of **Homer** (c. 800–700 BC), the author of the *Iliad* and the *Odyssey*. Taking as an example Achilles' sorrowful reaction to the loss of his comrades in the *Iliad*, Plato complained that Homer portrayed death as an evil to be feared rather than as a reminder of the riches to follow in paradise.

THE GRIEF AND LAMENTATION FOUND IN HOMER ENCOURAGES RAGE AGAINST THE GODS WHICH, IN TURN, SUPPORTS THE ERRONEOUS VIEW THAT THE GODS ARE RESPONSIBLE FOR EVIL.

THE GODS ARE BLAMELESS, RESPONSIBILITY LIES WITH THE CHOOSER.

Painting as Imitation

Plato also viewed painting (i.e. wall painting) derogatively, as an imitative art based on the copying of Nature. He compared painting to a mirror.

PAINTING IS NO MORE SKILLED THAN TURNING A MIRROR ROUND AND ROUND TO CAPTURE THE IMAGE OF THE SUN AND HEAVENS AND THE EARTH.

For this reason, Plato argued that painting is "twice removed from the truth", not even achieving the status of carpenters' artefacts which, he asserted, represent the blueprint of the higher Forms at one remove.

Although Plato condemned art, he never entirely disassociated art from truth. Rather, he stated that art is a pale mirror, or poor copy, of the truth. However, in *The Sophist* (360 BC), he discussed a category entirely apart from the truth, which he termed "simulacrum".

I IDENTIFY "SOPHIST" PHILOSOPHERS AS SIMULACRAL.

THESE ARE PHILOSOPHERS WHO EMPLOY ARGUMENTS WHICH SEEM UTTERLY CONVINCING BUT ARE, IN FACT, DECEPTIVELY FALLACIOUS.

Plato derogatively likened the Sophist philosopher to a magician: "a cheat who imitates reality" (*The Sophist*). Today, the word *sophistry* refers to a specious or deliberately deceptive form of argument.

Subsequent philosophers, such as Friedrich Nietzsche, and postmodern philosophers influenced by him, for instance Gilles Deleuze and Jacques Derrida, saw Plato's arguments about the simulacrum as the Achilles heel in his philosophy.

IF THE SIMULACRUM EXISTS OUTSIDE TRUTH, THEN PLATO IS NO LONGER IN A POSITION TO JUDGE IT IN RELATION TO TRUTH, AND CANNOT DESCRIBE IT AS FALSE!

Following Nietzsche, as we will see, postmodern philosophers nullified the opposition between truth and falsity. This in turn led to a re-evaluation of art's relation – or non-relation – to truth.

Deception is Truth, Truth Deception

The postmodernist critique of Plato was anticipated in classical times in a celebrated story told by the Roman scholar **Pliny the Elder** (23–79 AD) in his *Natural History*. Pliny described a competition between the painters Zeuxis and Parrhasios during the 5th century BC. Zeuxis painted a bunch of grapes so lifelike that they attracted the birds.

BUT I TRIUMPHED OVER HIM BY PAINTING A VEIL SO DECEPTIVE THAT ZEUXIS TURNED TO ME AND SAID ---

WELL, AND NOW DRAW ASIDE THE VEIL AND SHOW WHAT YOU HAVE PAINTED BEHIND IT.

WHEREAS ZEUXIS FOOLED THE BIRDS, PARRHASSIOS DECEIVED HIS FELLOW HUMAN BEINGS.

Plato always maintained that truth and falsity are opposed. This idea is perpetuated in the confusion arising from Zeuxis' painting. But Parrhasios contradicts this notion by revealing that deception is the truth, and vice versa. The French psychoanalyst Jacques Lacan was particularly fond of this story, and quoted it in his seminars during the 1960s and 70s.

Aristotle's *Poetics*

The *Poetics* (c. 335 BC) by the Greek philosopher **Aristotle** (384–322 BC) offered the most extensive analysis of art after Plato and served as a riposte to his condemnation of art. The *Poetics* laid the foundations for modern aesthetics.

IT FOCUSES NOT SO MUCH ON THE RELATIONSHIP BETWEEN ART, MORALITY AND TRUTH, AS PLATO DID ---

--- BUT RATHER ON THE STATUS AND INTERACTION OF PLEASURE, UNDERSTANDING AND EMOTION IN THE EXPERIENCE OF WORKS OF ART.

In addition, the *Poetics* explored what the relationship of works of art to reality might entail.

As with Plato, Aristotle's ideas about art made use of the concept of mimesis, or imitation.

BUT MY INTERPRETATION OF THIS CONCEPT DIFFERS SIGNIFICANTLY FROM PLATO'S.

I AM NOT INTERESTED IN EVALUATING ART IN TERMS OF ITS DEGREE OF TRUTH OR MORAL WORTH.

Aristotle rejected Plato's idea of art as a distorting mirror of reality. Instead he analysed art in terms of its ability to engender emotion – especially emotions of pleasure and pain.

17

Art and the Audience

Aristotle argued that the mimetic structure of art is embedded in the interaction between the work of art – poetry, drama, painting, sculpture, music and dance – and the audience. He stressed the fact that works of art have their own structures and forms which are independent of structures and forms in reality.

PLAYS REVOLVE AROUND PLOT INVOLVING CHARACTERS AND ACTION ---

--- WHILE MUSIC IS BASED ON STRUCTURES OF TONE, RHYTHMS AND MELODIES.

Since art has its own internal sense of structure and organization, Aristotle argued that it has a **fictional** status, rather than a **false** status as Plato had done.

Art and Reality

Although art possesses its own independent structures, Aristotle proposed that it is understood, evaluated and, ultimately, appreciated by the audience through a range of concepts derived from experience and life.

IN POETRY AND TRAGEDY WE ENCOUNTER NOTIONS OF PURPOSE AND CHOICE, SUCCESS AND FAILURE, PROSPERITY AND SUFFERING, GOOD AND EVIL, GUILT AND INNOCENCE.

Aristotle argued that the audience bring to bear these issues upon the work of art and, in turn, are affected by its expression of them.

Aristotle maintained that the fictional status of art makes it possible to appreciate and enjoy things which are, in reality, unattractive or painful.

WE TAKE PLEASURE IN CONTEMPLATING THE MOST PRECISELY RENDERED IMAGES EVEN OF THINGS WHOSE ACTUAL SIGHT WE FIND PAINFUL, SUCH AS THE FORMS OF THE BASEST ANIMALS AND OF CORPSES.

The experience of a work of art is different from reality, but its emotional effect is dependent upon its relationship to reality. Similarly, the material form of works of art – colours, shapes, words, rhythms, choreographic patterns – are also rooted in reality.

Catharsis

Using his ideas about the fictional status of art, Aristotle made a particular study of the emotions aroused by tragic drama. This formed the basis for his theory of "catharsis". Aristotle perceived how tragic drama draws on the audience's feelings of pity and fear – it was common for Athenian spectators to weep openly at stage performances.

THESE FEELINGS ARE AROUSED PARTICULARLY WHEN THE HERO SUFFERS A SIGNIFICANT REVERSAL OF FORTUNES ---

--- SUCH AS WHEN OEDIPUS, IN SOPHOCLES' DRAMA OEDIPUS REX, DISCOVERS THAT JOCASTA, HIS WIFE, IS IN FACT HIS MOTHER.

THE TRAGEDY IS COMPOUNDED BY THE FACT THAT THE MESSENGER WHO REVEALS OEDIPUS' TRUE IDENTITY INITIALLY CAME TO DELIVER JOYOUS NEWS.

Catharsis is the feeling of sympathy aroused in the audience for Oedipus in this tragic moment of reversal. Aristotle argued that the fictional status of the play creates a sense of distance between the spectator and the tragic hero, and that because of this it is possible to enjoy tragedy and take aesthetic pleasure in it.

Medieval Aesthetics

As Christianity arose in the West, replacing paganism (the Emperor Constantine converted to Christianity in 337 AD), aesthetics and the problem of beauty were subsumed within theological debates. These debates revolved around questions such as whether God created the universe from nothing.

A further conflict raged over how to accommodate God, considered to be an absolutely perfect Being, with his imperfect creation, Man, immured in sin following the Fall of Adam and Eve from paradise.

THIS CONFLICT WAS EMBEDDED WITHIN THE CLASSICAL DISTINCTION BETWEEN THE METAPHYSICAL, TRANSCENDENT REALM OF THE ABSOLUTE, AND THE SENSORY, CORPOREAL REALM INHABITED BY MAN.

The Theological Time-bomb

Theologians struggled to reconcile this distinction, all the while dimly aware that the existence of moral impurity (represented by Man) compromised God's own absolute purity and, indeed, his very existence. **St Augustine** (354–430), a born-again convert, and **St Thomas Aquinas** (1225–74), a Dominican friar, adapted the philosophies of Plato and Aristotle in an attempt to fulfil Christian requirements and resolve the paradoxes of metaphysics.

THIS THEOLOGICAL CONUNDRUM WAS LIKE A BOMB WAITING TO GO OFF IN THE LAP OF CHRISTIAN BELIEF.

I FINALLY DETONATED IT AT THE END OF THE 19TH CENTURY WHEN I DECLARED THAT GOD IS DEAD.

Friedrich Nietzsche

The Beauty of Order

Like Plato, Augustine believed in an underlying metaphysical form and order to the universe. For Augustine, this belief in metaphysics was associated with God, and he considered anything possessing a sense of order and unity to be beautiful, as it reflected a higher order. Augustine was particularly attracted to objects and forms with a sense of numerical order and proportion.

Sidestepping the traditional Christian association of sensual pleasure with immorality, Augustine connected the appreciation of beauty to reason and the mind. Hence his interest in mathematical proportion. He considered the pleasure associated with smell or taste as base, since it supposedly lacked any intellectual qualities.

ANYONE WOULD BE LAUGHED AT IF HE SHOULD SAY THAT SOMETHING SMELLS REASONABLY OR TASTES REASONABLY.

Departing marginally from Plato, Augustine was a little more generous towards artists and playwrights, stating that it was not necessarily their fault that art was incapable of representing higher truths.

Thomas Aquinas

Whereas classical culture, both Greek and Roman, was a living culture for St Augustine, it had largely disappeared from view by the 10th century owing to a lack of knowledge of Greek and a disapproval of pagan religion. However, in the 11th century the texts of Plato and Aristotle became available again in translation, and in the 13th century it was to these writers that Thomas Aquinas turned for inspiration.

FOLLOWING ARISTOTLE, I EXPLORED THE RELATIONSHIP BETWEEN THE PERCEIVER AND THE EXPERIENCE OF BEAUTY.

This contrasted with Augustine's neo-Platonic philosophy which excluded the perceiver from consideration and viewed sensual beauty as an imitation of God's own beauty.

Beauty and Cognition

According to Aquinas, beauty produces a harmonious and restful state which is derived not so much from visual experience as from the activity of **cognition** (the faculty of knowing) in the perception of beauty.

COGNITION ABSTRACTS THE ESSENTIAL FORM OF THINGS AND THIS PRODUCES A HARMONIOUS STATE OF MIND AND BEING.

As with St Augustine, Aquinas' theory of beauty and cognition reveals his desire to associate the experience of beauty with the intellect rather than with the senses, thereby giving it an acceptable status within Christian theology. Following this, Aquinas stated that just as the Son of God is associated with a spiritual light, so the intellect is light and splendid.

While poetry and music were objects of discussion in the medieval period, they were subsumed within the concept of "the seven liberal arts", comprising Grammar, Dialectic and Rhetoric, Arithmetic, Music, Geometry and Astronomy.

Art as Religious Instruction

A level of scepticism ran through medieval culture towards the legacy of Roman art because of its association with idolatry. But at certain times in the medieval period, images were defended as having a necessary didactic (teaching) function.

HE WHO SHOWS REVERENCE TO THE IMAGE SHOWS REVERENCE TO THE SUBJECT REPRESENTED IN IT.

In the Byzantine era in Constantinople (4th century AD to the 15th century), art was considered important as a priestly – and frequently austere – symbol of divine power. In the West by the end of the medieval period, between the 14th and 16th centuries, art was more openly embraced as an aid to religious instruction. Even the great Gothic cathedrals had an illustrative function, underlining the idea of God as architect of the universe.

Art and Melancholy

Medieval doctrine believed that mental and physiological states were governed by four humours: the sanguine, the choleric, the phlegmatic and the melancholic. The last of these was associated with withdrawal, depression and madness. However, in the late 15th century, Neo-Platonist scholars such as the Florentine **Marsilio Ficino** (1433–99) asserted that the melancholic condition was important for intellectual creativity and, ultimately, a sense of spirituality.

MELANCHOLY IS ASSOCIATED WITH THE SOLITUDE REQUIRED BY SCHOLARS AND ARTISTS FOR STUDY AND ARTISTIC ENDEAVOUR.

The School of Night

The idea of melancholy was taken up by Elizabethan poets in the late 16th century, including **Edmund Spenser** (1552–99), **George Chapman** (1560–1634), **Walter Ralegh** (1554–1618) and other members of "the School of Night". The lyricist **John Dowland** (1563–1626) devoted a number of songs to melancholy. Dowland's "In Darkness Let Me Dwell" includes the lines:

> Wedded to my woes and bedded to my tomb,
> O let me living die, till death do come.

In *Melencolia I* (1514), the German artist **Albrecht Dürer** (1471–1528) produced the definitive image of melancholy. Poised between activity and idleness, Dürer's angel reflects upon the dark, Saturnine qualities overshadowing intellectual work and genius.

Renaissance Aesthetics

Writers on art in Italy during the Renaissance (which lasted from approximately the 13th to the 17th centuries) revived the classical conception of mimesis originating from Plato and Aristotle. Literally, mimesis means imitation, and it is the root of the word "mime". The architect **Leone Battista Alberti** (1404–72) in his treatise *On Painting* (1435) employed the concept of mimesis in relation to the pursuit of naturalistic effects and the look of the "real" in art.

Painting as Philosophy

The notebooks of **Leonardo da Vinci** (1452–1519) reveal that he conceived of painting as a branch of natural philosophy. Leonardo attributed importance to what can be learned by means of the eye – which he called "the window of the soul". Unlike Plato, Leonardo placed great value on the idea of art acting as a mirror to Nature and reality. This was because he believed that Nature was part of divine creation.

Leonardo's interest both in the way things appear to sight and in the laws of Nature led him to study anatomy, physics, geometry and perspective.

The Rise of the Bourgeoisie

The social and economic context of the Renaissance lay in the expansion of the Capitalist market and the rise of the bourgeoisie. These conditions led to a greater sense of individual competitiveness in economic terms, with artists vying for patrons and commissions. Artists like **Raphael** (1483–1520) acted as directors of artistic projects with big commercial studios and a host of assistants producing the actual work.

DIRECTOR

THIS ENABLED PAINTINGS TO BE EXECUTED WITH A SENSE OF AMBITION AND ON A SCALE NOT PREVIOUSLY ENVISAGED.

The Lives of the Artists

A new genre of biography arose in the Renaissance, the best known of which was *The Lives of the Most Excellent Italian Architects, Painters and Sculptors* (1550) by **Giorgio Vasari** (1511–74), detailing some of the most renowned Renaissance artists' lives and careers, including Giotto, Leonardo and Michelangelo.

VASARI'S LIVES ELEVATED THE SOCIAL POSITION OF THE ARTIST.

THIS REFLECTED A NEW CONCEPTION OF ARCHITECTURE, PAINTING AND SCULPTURE AS "LIBERAL ARTS" RATHER THAN MANUAL OR TECHNICAL CRAFTS.

Related to this change, ideas of artistic creativity and originality were discussed for the first time since the classical period, although the artist's ability was assessed according to original ways of representing religious and metaphysical ideals.

The Classical Episteme

The French philosopher **Michel Foucault** (1926–84) argued in his book *The Order of Things* (1966) that the culture and ideas of the Renaissance and the period immediately following it were part of a network of knowledge and values which belong to "the Classical episteme" (an episteme is a system of knowledge).

The Subject

In keeping with Christian ideas of a Supreme Being (God) and absolutist ideas of the sovereign king, the Classical episteme posits an ideal of a transcendent, objective Mind or Subject. In painting during this period, especially in southern Europe, the Subject stands literally and metaphorically before the pictured world like an omnipotent God. In Raphael's *School of Athens* (1510–11), for example, a central space is reserved for the Subject, who is both viewer and addressee of the painting.

In southern European painting the idea of a sovereign viewing Subject is supported by the use of perspective, the invention of which is often credited to Alberti. As he stated in his treatise of 1435: "The function of the painter is to draw given bodies in such a way that at a fixed distance and with a certain position what you see represented appears to be in relief and just like those bodies."

All the objects in this painting, Raphael's *Marriage of the Virgin* (1504), are scaled in proportion to each other within a box-like space. The perspective lines are constructed in such a way that the viewer walks into and completes the represented scene, becoming essential and central to it.

The Sovereign Eye

In *The Order of Things*, Foucault proposed that the masterpiece of **Diego Velázquez** (1599–1660), *Las Meninas* (*The Ladies-in-Waiting*, 1656–7), marks the zenith of the ideology of the sovereign eye or Subject in Western culture. The subject-matter of Velázquez's painting is a depiction of the five-year-old Infanta Margarita Teresa, who is seen in the foreground accompanied by her supplicant ladies-in-waiting and the court dwarfs. Behind the Infanta stand several courtiers and the Queen's chamberlain. To the Infanta's side at the back of the room the reflection of King Philip IV and his wife is visible in a mirror.

The King and Queen are positioned outside the painting and occupy the same place as the viewer. The implication of *Las Meninas* is that the Infanta and her entourage are visiting her parents, who are having their portrait painted by Velázquez (he has depicted himself in the foreground to the left, working at his easel).

THIS DISPLACEMENT OF THE KING AND QUEEN FROM THE MAIN SCENE MIGHT SEEM TO ANNOUNCE THE BREAK-UP OF THE CLASSICAL EPISTEME.

BUT VISION IN LAS MENINAS REMAINS ENTIRELY CIRCUMSCRIBED BY THE KING AND QUEEN: WE SEE EXACTLY WHAT THEY SEE.

Et in Arcadia Ego

A similar ideology to that of Velázquez's painting is evident in *Arcadian Shepherds* (1638) by **Nicolas Poussin** (1594–1665), a work analysed by the French art historian Louis Marin in 1980. The eponymous shepherds discover an epigram on a tomb which reads "Et in Arcadia Ego".

The legend informs the innocent and contented shepherds of mortality. Despite its stark message, the painting contains a strategic device which flattered the Subject, in this case the commissioner and owner of the painting, Cardinal Rospigliosi. The shepherd who deciphers the legend points to a letter "r", the first letter of the Cardinal's name, and this letter is inscribed at the exact centre of the painting.

The Imperialist Subject

The paintings of Velázquez and Poussin upheld the idea of a Subject in control of the visual field and, by implication, the world. This ideology of the Subject ultimately stemmed from Imperialist societies like those of ancient Egypt. Imperialist societies were governed by an essentially aggressive and militaristic attitude towards outside cultures, which they regarded as potential objects of conquest and economic gain. At their most extreme, they prohibited intermarriage with other cultures in order to preserve the "purity" of their own race.

The concept of the Subject in these instances of Imperialism is constructed around the ideology of racial purity.

Capitalism and the Other

With the rise of Capitalism in the West from the Renaissance onwards, a different attitude towards outside cultures developed. While Imperialist conquests persisted, forming the basis of the British, French and Prussian empires, economic relations with non-Western societies were encouraged in order to expand both the production of commodities and the Capitalist market.

IMPERIALIST ECONOMIC RELATIONS WITH OTHER CULTURES AND RACES ARE SOLELY AGGRESSIVE.

BUT CAPITALISM PROMOTES ECONOMIC EXCHANGE – SO LONG AS IT LEADS TO FINANCIAL PROFIT.

In contemporary philosophy, the issue of the Subject's relation to that which is different is termed "alterity", which is derived from the Latin *alteritas*, meaning "being other". Alterity bears not just upon issues of race and gender, but on all forms of difference. In this context, the Other designates not simply an idea of divergency, but of an absolute difference that is by definition unknowable and, therefore, **unrepresentable**.

ANY RELATION WITH THE OTHER IS ALSO, BY IMPLICATION, UNREPRESENTABLE, LEAVING NO ROOM FOR A CONTROLLING SUBJECT.

Jacques Derrida

The Enlightenment

Throughout Europe in the 18th century there arose a wholesale questioning of Imperialist and absolutist ideologies. Religion, too, was regarded with scepticism; one of the consequences of which was that the Prussian philosopher **Immanuel Kant** (1724–1804) declared that philosophy had no business dealing with the question of God and his purported existence. Kant, and other European philosophers such as **Denis Diderot** (1713–84) and **Jean-Jacques Rousseau** (1712–78), embraced a new sense of secular "Enlightenment". Nevertheless, the issue of alterity remained a sticking point.

Kant's Critical Philosophy

Kant formulated his "critical" philosophy (encompassing the three *Critiques* of *Pure Reason*, *Practical Reason* and *Judgement*) during the 1780s. In answer to the question, What is knowledge?, he proposed that knowledge is formed out of an exchange or "synthesis" with the Other. Kant's great achievement lay in his recognition that new knowledge is dependent upon an exchange with **what cannot be known**, otherwise this knowledge would not be genuinely new. But, despite this recognition, Kant still preserved the idea of a controlling Subject capable of formulating the conditions of a projected body of knowledge.

I CALL THIS THE "A PRIORI", MEANING WHAT CAN ALWAYS BE GIVEN IN ADVANCE.

The Critique of Judgement

The third *Critique*, the *Critique of Judgement* (1790), was one of the first philosophical tracts devoted exclusively to the study of sensory and emotional experience which became known as aesthetics. Whereas previously, from Plato to the Enlightenment, beauty had been gauged according to the ideals of the metaphysical world and their traces within Nature or the mind, Kant acknowledged – at least initially – that the appreciation of beauty is entirely **subjective**.

SOME PEOPLE MAY ADORE THE LOOK OF A ROSE, WHILE OTHERS MAY NOT.

NEVERTHELESS, I INSIST THAT ALL DISCUSSION ABOUT BEAUTY HAS A UNIVERSAL DIMENSION ---

--- SINCE, ULTIMATELY, IT IS ADDRESSED TO A PROJECTED COMMUNITY OF ENGAGED PARTICIPANTS, THE "SENSUS COMMUNIS".

Although Kant stated that emotional experience is not to do with a concept, or non-cognitive, he still maintained that beauty consists of a harmonious correspondence between experience and the intellect.

The Sublime

Following his analysis of beauty, Kant investigated what the emotional experience of synthesis with the Other is like. For this purpose, he re-employed the concept of **the sublime**, which had fallen into disuse since the Greek rhetorician Longinus in the mid-1st century AD. The sublime is an experience of being overwhelmed and of losing control. As a way of illustrating this, Kant referred to the sense of vertigo induced by vast architectural edifices, such as the Pyramids or the interior of St Peter's in Rome – "the mathematical sublime". Similarly, he spoke of the mortal fear provoked by wild nature …

Nevertheless, Kant insisted that the sublime is not dependent upon an object, because it exceeds the grasp of both cognition and feeling: "it" – the sublime – is unrepresentable. The consequence of Kant's conception is that the controlling Subject disappears in the wake of an experiential excess. But Kant withdrew from this conclusion.

I MAINTAIN THAT THE EXPERIENCE OF THE SUBLIME GENERATES AN UNEXPECTED FEELING OF DELIGHT AS A SENSE OF SPACE AND TIME BECOMES ENLARGED.

Kant introduced the feeling of delight in order to assign a positive value to the experience of the sublime, and so safeguard the Subject from being irrevocably changed by it. In effect, Kant suggested that the Other is always less than the Subject might justifiably fear. This move to protect the Subject was commensurate with Capitalist ideology which centres around the idea of the Subject.

Universal Reason

In his theory of the sublime, Kant daringly suggested that any encounter with what is different and unknown is, by definition, unrepresentable. This idea influenced later philosophers such as Nietzsche, Heidegger and Bataille as well as postmodern philosophers. Eventually however, Kant tried to qualify his foray into the unknown, saying that the sublime is, ultimately, governed by a quasi-religious concept called "Reason".

I EQUATE REASON WITH MY BELIEF IN MAN'S SUPERIOR INTELLIGENCE.

REASON GUARANTEES THAT AESTHETIC JUDGEMENTS ABOUT BEAUTY AND THE SUBLIME ARE FREE AND DISINTERESTED BECAUSE THEY ARE RULED BY THE SUPERIORITY OF THE MIND.

Kant's ideas about the "disinterestedness" – or purity and freedom – of aesthetic judgements influenced both Romantic and Modernist aesthetics (see pages 73–7), although they were challenged by the major triumvirate of modern philosophers: Nietzsche, Freud and Marx.

The Unknowable

In the *Critique of Pure Reason* (1780) Kant stated that there are limits to knowledge and that there are "things" which escape its competence. He named this excess "Noumenon", meaning that which is unknowable. Kant proposed that the Noumenon "marks the limits of sensible knowledge". He did not realize that the concept of Noumenon renders limits non-existent and compromises the very possibility of "sensible knowledge" altogether, since it is impossible to define knowledge in relation to what is unknown and unrepresentable.

KNOWLEDGE

NOUMENON

THIS WAS A PARADOX WHICH KANT NEVER RESOLVED, AND WHICH I, HEGEL, INHERITED.

Hegel and the Universal Consciousness

Like Kant, the German philosopher **G.W.F. Hegel** (1770–1831) recognized that there are excessive – and, therefore, unrepresentable – experiences which are fundamental to emotions and human existence. While Kant named these experiences as sublime, Hegel thought that they must be categorised in terms of non-being.

I ASSOCIATE NON-BEING WITH DEATH AND THE FINITUDE OF MANKIND AND THE UNIVERSE.

Hegel was a Christian philosopher and, as such, he believed that death and finitude are ordained by God and are part of his divine plan.

I INHERITED THE AGE—OLD THEOLOGICAL PROBLEM OF HOW TO RECONCILE GOD, WHO IS AN IMMORTAL BEING, WITH FINITUDE AND NON—BEING.

Hegel's solution was to come up with the proposal that mankind would eventually recognize that it is its own destiny to be unable to represent non-being. This would be accompanied by a new consciousness or Spirit which embraced this condition as God-given

Symbolic, Classical, Romantic

Hegel believed that the historical process leading towards the dawn of Spirit is divided into three major phases, which are reflected in the history of art. Symbolic art points towards Spirit without being able to adequately represent it. This art takes a representational form (humans or animals), or an allegorical form. The next stage is Classical art, by which Hegel meant specifically Greek sculpture.

THE FINAL STAGE IS THAT OF THE CHRISTIAN RELIGION (WHICH I CALL "ROMANTIC" ART).

For Hegel, these phases of art represent an inexorable movement towards a recognition that Man cannot represent or conceptualize non-being.

Hegel believed that this recognition would mean that art was no longer needed.

ART IS THE SENSUOUS APPEARING OF THE IDEA BUT IT CANNOT FULLY COMPREHEND IT.

CONSEQUENTLY, I ANNOUNCE THE IMMINENT END OF ART.

Out of the ruins of Man's limitation to conceptualize non-being, Hegel salvaged a sense of purpose: for him, this limitation marked the realization that non-being should be held in awe as proof of a divine intellect capable of reconciling opposites within itself. However, Hegel's appeal to a divine and transcendent order as a way of synthesizing all forms of experience – including even those which can't be represented – came under increasing attack by philosophers as the 19th century proceeded.

The Origins of Modern Aesthetics: Nietzsche, Freud and Marx

Whereas Hegel hung on to a sense of a divine plan structuring all experiences, even those which are excessive or unrepresentable, the work of **Friedrich Nietzsche** (1844–1900), **Sigmund Freud** (1856–1939) and **Karl Marx** (1818–83) attempted to explain experience without recourse to theology or to received ideas about rationality and reason. Above all, this meant overturning traditional notions of the Subject as being defined by, and conceived as part of, a greater whole.

I PURSUED THE RADICAL CONSEQUENCES OF THE CONCEPT OF ALTERITY FIRST TOUCHED ON BY KANT IN HIS THEORIES OF THE SUBLIME AND THE NOUMENON.

BOTH MARX AND I CRITIQUED NOTIONS OF CONTROL AND CONSCIOUSNESS WITHIN THE SPHERES OF ECONOMICS AND PSYCHOANALYSIS, RESPECTIVELY.

AS A CONSEQUENCE, THE IDEA OF A UNIFIED SUBJECT IN CONTROL OF THEIR EXPERIENCES BEGAN TO FALL APART.

In their different ways, this triumvirate of writers founded both modern and postmodern philosophy and aesthetics.

Nietzsche and the Revaluation of All Values

Nietzsche daringly dispensed with the purported opposition between the Subject and the Other, the vestiges of which were maintained by Hegel.

In Nietzsche's philosophy – which he described as "the revaluation of all values" – the unrepresentable defies all conceptual oppositions and fixed representations, including the opposition between truth and falsity, since what is absolutely false (Plato's conception of the simulacrum) is not even comparable with the truth. For Nietzsche, writing in *Twilight of the Idols* (1888), this realization marks "the end of the longest error" and "the high point of humanity".

Apollonian and Dionysian Energy

In Nietzsche's opinion, the potential for real creative energy in society had been stifled for several millennia – since the early Greek writers such as Homer and the tragedians Aeschylus and Sophocles in the 5th century BC. Nietzsche appreciated their writing as possessing a libidinal energy expressed in rhythm and musicality, and he identified two opposing but mutually enhancing tendencies composing this energy: the **Apollonian** tendency towards form and images, and the **Dionysian** tendency towards intoxication and excess.

I PARTICULARLY VALUE THE LATTER TENDENCY AS A LIBIDINAL OR INSTINCTUAL ENERGY ARISING FROM THE UNCONSCIOUS THAT OPPOSES FIXED VALUES AND FORMS.

Since the Dionysian tendency embraced conflicts, Nietzsche believed that it was capable of superseding moral agendas and the consequent inhibiting fear of perceived threats from the "outside". "Beauty" in Nietzsche's revised terms signalled the collapse of all conceptually and morally determined oppositions.

"BEAUTY" EXISTS OUTSIDE ALL ORDERS OF RANK, BECAUSE IN BEAUTY OPPOSITES ARE TAMED, MOREOVER WITHOUT TENSION.

THAT VIOLENCE IS NO LONGER NEEDED, THAT EVERYTHING FOLLOWS, OBEYS, SO EASILY AND SO PLEASANTLY – THAT IS WHAT DELIGHTS THE ARTIST'S WILL TO POWER.

For Nietzsche, the "will to power" was the ability to embrace change – and what is new or different – and convert it into creative energy. The idea of the will to power was later misinterpreted by the Nazis in Germany in the 1930s, who thought it reflected their own ideology of Aryan supremacy.

The Intoxication of Change

In Nietzsche's vision, humanity has the potential to become selfless and fluid, perpetually engaged in overthrowing and changing values before they fall back into the paradoxes of metaphysics. In his notebook in 1888, Nietzsche jotted down a sketch of this intoxicating process.

Freud and Psychoanalysis

Working in Vienna at the heart of the Austro-Hungarian empire, Sigmund Freud undermined the idea of a Subject who is supposedly conscious and in control of his thoughts and actions by establishing the notion of the **unconscious**.

THE UNIFIED SUBJECT IS AN ILLUSORY PRODUCT OF THE EGO ARISING OUT OF A FAILURE TO RECOGNIZE THE DEEP CONFLICTS OF THE PSYCHE.

These conflicts have their roots in familial relationships and the so-called "Oedipus complex" which inculcates in the child divisive feelings of love and hatred towards parents and siblings.

According to Freud, the formation of the Subject's individual psyche occurs through a consciousness of gender. However, this can bring with it feelings of anxiety, envy and fear which are often buried in the unconscious. For Freud, the purpose of the psychoanalytic treatment is to help the patient to recognize sexual difference and to explore their repressed conflictual feelings.

Freud's "invention" of the unconscious highlighted the fact that there is more in the psyche than consciousness is aware of at any one time. There are unresolved feelings and experiences in the unconscious stemming from childhood and influencing adulthood.

FOR FREUD, SUBJECTIVITY IS FRAGMENTED AND DISCONTINUOUS.

In the modern period this sense of fragmented subjectivity was represented in the collage methods employed by **Pablo Picasso** (1881–1973) and **Georges Braque** (1882–1963) in Cubism and the free-form literary style of **James Joyce** (1882–1941).

Sublimation

Consciousness consists of a constant struggle to make sense of fragmented experiences and bring them into form through understanding and language. With this idea in mind, Freud developed a theory of artistic representation and transformation which he termed "sublimation". Sublimation gives form to repressed unconscious feelings through narratives and representations.

Freud felt that the statue illustrated the prophet's renunciation of his feelings of anger at his people in order to save the symbol which defined his community, the tablets of the Ten Commandments. Moses is seen tucking the tablets safely under his arm after losing his grip on them for a moment in his initial state of anger.

On a number of occasions, Freud analysed art as a symptom of unconscious desires and fears. In an essay on Leonardo da Vinci (1910), Freud described how he was particularly struck by the bizarre effect of the two women in Leonardo's cartoon for *St Anne with the Madonna and Two Others* (c. 1498), in which it appears "as if two heads were growing from a single body".

AT FIRST, THIS MONSTROUS HYDRA-LIKE IMAGE UNDERLYING THE COMPOSITION OF THE TWO WOMEN MIGHT NOT BE NOTICED. ONCE SEEN, IT REVEALS THE EMERGENCE OF LEONARDO'S UNCONSCIOUS FEAR OF WOMEN.

Marx and the Alienation of Capitalism

Although Marx's writings were concerned principally with political economy, they had profound consequences in the modern period for conceptualizing the conditions and possibilities of artistic production and, more widely, human experience. Marx argued in the *Grundrisse, or Critique of Political Economy* (1857) and *Capital* (1867) that in modern, Capitalist societies Man is alienated both from himself and from his human possibilities.

It was on the basis of this analysis that Marx called for a revolutionary change to the world.

Art and the Bourgeoisie

The few remarks that Marx made about art are linked to his critique of bourgeois values and ideas. Marx argued that the enduring appeal of Greek art is not that such art is timeless, as the bourgeoisie claim.

THE IDEA OF TIMELESSNESS SUSTAINS THE ECONOMIC VALUE OF ART WHILE ALSO CONCEALING THE HISTORICAL CIRCUMSTANCES IN WHICH ART IS PRODUCED ---

--- AND THE CLASS DIFFERENCES EXISTING IN THESE CIRCUMSTANCES.

Marx stated that the real reason why Greek art continues to be enjoyed is that it was produced at the dawn of Western civilization, during its "childhood". Thus, a certain nostalgia exists for the products of that "innocent" time.

Marx believed that mythology was important for the Greeks to make sense of unpredictable natural forces. But what, he asked, is the function of art in the modern period? He argued that it can no longer have the same function as in Greek society since mankind has now gained control over nature through technology.

THEREFORE, MODERN ART REQUIRES THE ARTIST TO HAVE A FANTASY INDEPENDENT OF MYTHOLOGY.

Marx indicated that this capability for "independent fantasy" involved an imaginative ability to represent the world in ways that science and technology cannot, and a capacity to grasp universal meanings concerning class inequality.

Aestheticism

During the same period as Nietzsche was writing in Germany, a different, more patrician, notion of ancient Greek culture – Hellenism – was explored in England. In this context, Hellenism stood for a life absorbed by art and beauty beyond questions of morality or ethics. **Walter Pater** (1839–94) declared that the aim of life is "to burn always with a hard, gemlike flame", and to fill every moment with passionate experience. In the conclusion to his work *The Renaissance: Studies in Art and Poetry* (1873), Pater celebrated experience as an end in itself.

Pater's philosophy gave rise to the idea of the "aesthete", portrayed by **Oscar Wilde** (1854–1900) as the dandy Lord Henry Wotton in his novel *The Picture of Dorian Gray* (1891), which is about the desire to stay young and beautiful. Wilde himself appeared to adhere to the ideals of the aesthete when he wrote provocatively in the preface to his novel:

However, the downfall of the eponymous hero of *Dorian Gray* demonstrates the moribundity and self-destructiveness of a life dedicated to sensual gratification beyond the moral bounds of conscience.

Wilde's statement in the preface to *Dorian Gray* that "All art is useless" is often seen as the rallying cry of the ideology of "art for art's sake". This is the idea that the work of art is separate from, or transcends, ideological, political and moral concerns.

In the absence of a specifically religious art in the late 19th and 20th centuries, "art for art's sake" took on a quasi-religious significance.

Modernist Aesthetics

Wilde's brand of aestheticism was part of a wider ideology which claimed that the work of art is autonomous and independent of materialist concerns. Gathering momentum in the 20th century, this ideology pervaded a substantial part of the discourse of art during the modern period.

WE MODERNISTS EXPLAIN OUR ART THROUGH AN EMPHASIS ON FORMAL AND SPIRITUAL VALUES.

Roger Fry (1866–1934)

Modernist ideas that experience exists in and of itself are developed by the painter **Wassily Kandinsky** (1866–1944) in his theory of "synaesthesia". Kandinsky believed in the correspondences of the senses (synaesthesia), with the result that colour was seen to have a musical effect.

COLOUR IS THE KEYBOARD, THE EYES ARE THE HAMMERS, THE SOUL IS THE PIANO WITH MANY STRINGS.

THE ARTIST IS THE HAND THAT PLAYS, TOUCHING ONE KEY OR ANOTHER PURPOSIVELY, TO CAUSE VIBRATIONS IN THE SOUL.

Such ideas of the purely experiential nature of the work of art were seen to oppose bourgeois materialism. However, in some exceptional cases, modernist artists were not afraid to express their allegiance to bourgeois values. The painter **Henri Matisse** (1869–1954) declared in 1908:

I DREAM OF AN ART OF BALANCE, PURITY AND SERENITY WHICH MIGHT BE FOR EVERY MENTAL WORKER, BE HE BUSINESSMAN OR WRITER, LIKE A GOOD ARMCHAIR IN WHICH TO REST.

Romanticism

The idea of the work of art's autonomy was derived from Kant's idea of the freedom and "disinterestedness" of aesthetic judgements and, subsequently, from the Romantic movement in the late 18th and early 19th centuries.

The story goes that the painter **Joseph Turner** (1775–1851) tied himself to a ship's mast in order to witness a storm, while the French Romantic artist **Théodore Géricault** (1789–1824) frequently risked his life riding recklessly in order to understand horses, as well as Man's relation to them.

Some aspects of the Romantics' excessive behaviour was self-indulgent and macho, but it was also linked to a deep sense of fate and tragedy which, like Kant's initial ideas about the sublime, emphasized humanity's vulnerability and powerlessness. This sense of fate was often figured through a grim portrayal of Man's struggle with Nature, as in the paintings *The Raft of the Medusa* (1819) by Géricault and *The Wreck of Hope* (1824) by **Caspar David Friedrich** (1774–1840).

No less fatalistic are the novels of **Thomas Hardy** (1840–1928) in which, as in *Jude the Obscure* (1895), the damp Wessex countryside provides the bleak counterpoint to the narrative's tragedy.

Marxist Aesthetics in the 1920s and 30s

Throughout the 20th century, writers of the Marxist intellectual tradition criticized Modernist aesthetics and ideology. Their argument was that art, and human experience generally, is not autonomous but is affected and shaped by **ideology** (Capitalist values and beliefs).

MARXISTS ARGUE THAT EITHER ART SUSTAINS IDEOLOGY OR IT CAN BE CRITICAL OF IT.

A major issue within Marxist debates has been concerned with how art achieves such criticality and how to portray the interests of the oppressed under Capitalism.

Marxist debates about art became pronounced in Germany and Russia in the 1920s and 30s. This was a period of economic crisis in both countries. In Germany, politics were polarized between right-wing factions and the Communist party, while in Russia the Revolution of 1917 brought the Communist party to power.

Lukács and Critical Realism

Working in Moscow from 1933 until 1945, the Hungarian Marxist **Georg Lukács** (1885–1971) developed a theory of "Critical Realism" with respect to literature. Lukács admired narrative novelists such as **Cervantes** (1547–1616), **Balzac** (1799–1850), **Dickens** (1812–70), **Gorky** (1868–1936), **Tolstoy** (1828–1910) and **Thomas Mann** (1875–1955).

I PARTICULARLY ADMIRE BALZAC.

I AGREE WITH MARX THAT BALZAC ANTICIPATED THE EMERGENCE OF KEY TYPICAL CHARACTERS UNDER THE REIGN OF NAPOLEON III FROM 1852 TO 1870.

Lukács believed that Balzac helped to establish a "realist" tradition of complex characterization which captured the underlying social processes at work in Capitalism. But his arguments were vehemently challenged by the German playwright **Bertolt Brecht** (1898–1956). Brecht argued that Lukács' position was not responsive to the new demands of the epoch.

WERE WE TO COPY THE STYLE OF THESE REALISTS, WE WOULD NO LONGER BE REALISTS.

FOR TIME FLOWS ON, METHODS BECOME EXHAUSTED, STIMULI NO LONGER WORK ---

WHAT WAS POPULAR YESTERDAY IS NOT TODAY, FOR THE PEOPLE TODAY ARE NOT WHAT THEY WERE YESTERDAY.

Corresponding to his definition of the popular, Brecht defined realism as: "discovering the causal complexes of society / unmasking the prevailing view of things as the view of those who are in power / writing from the standpoint of the class which offers the broadest solutions for the pressing difficulties in which human society is caught up / emphasizing the element of development / making possible the concrete, and making possible abstraction from it."

As a committed Marxist, Brecht wanted his audience to think about the political ramifications of his plays and not be complacent. In order to keep his audience on their toes, he constantly interjected different effects into the theatrical performance: narrators, music, choirs, newsreel clips, diagrams and multiple settings.

Communist Aesthetics

Following the Russian Revolution in 1917, Communists agreed that art should be appropriate to the needs of the proletariat. But there was much debate about what form this art should take. Underlying this debate lay different interpretations of the implications of Marx's notional division of society into a **base** and a **superstructure**.

Following Marx, **Lenin** (1870–1924) believed that the economic base of society, including the distribution of the means of production, determined its superstructure. But **Leon Trotsky** (1879–1940) believed that sometimes the superstructure, or elements within it, may be more advanced in revolutionary potential than the economic base. So art or literature may be of a revolutionary nature even though the economy is Capitalist.

IN A REVOLUTIONARY BREAK IN THE LIFE OF SOCIETY, THERE IS NO SIMULTANEOUSNESS AND NO SYMMETRY OF PROCESSES EITHER IN THE IDEOLOGY OF SOCIETY, OR IN ITS ECONOMIC STRUCTURE.

Socialist Realism

Under Stalin, debates about art's role and position within Russia were given short shrift. Opposed to Trotsky and the avant-garde, Soviet policy from the mid-1930s became increasingly conservative and looked to the 19th century for models of artistic style.

THE PARTY MUST MAKE USE OF ALL THE TECHNICAL ACHIEVEMENTS OF THE OLD MASTERS TO WORK OUT AN APPROPRIATE FORM, INTELLIGIBLE TO THE MILLIONS.

Pronouncements like these gave rise to the style known as Socialist Realism. The Party came to see avant-garde art as anathema to its aims.

Aesthetics in the Modern Era

Walter Benjamin

Opposed equally to simplistic right- and left-wing thinking, the German Marxist intellectual **Walter Benjamin** (1892–1940) made a series of important contributions in the 1930s to the debate on art's political efficacy. Benjamin was no advocate of propaganda or Socialist Realism, and nor did he believe that radicality lay in simply depicting poverty or oppression.

> THE BOURGEOIS APPARATUS OF PRODUCTION AND PUBLICATION CAN ASSIMILATE ASTONISHING QUALITIES OF REVOLUTIONARY THEMES ---

> --- INDEED, CAN PROPAGATE THEM WITHOUT CALLING ITS OWN EXISTENCE SERIOUSLY INTO QUESTION.

Like Brecht, Benjamin desired technical radicalism in art, with the aim of calling into question the accustomed ways in which ideas are represented and understood.

86

According to Benjamin, the major repressive technique of the bourgeoisie with respect to art is achieved by creating an "aura" about art, and ascribing to it notions of authenticity, uniqueness and originality. Benjamin believed that discussion of the work of art's beauty – if carried out to the exclusion of its social context – could also contribute to this false "aura".

BOURGEOIS SOCIETY TREATS WORKS OF ART AS IF THEY ARE A MYSTERIOUS SECRET TO BE WORSHIPPED ---

--- AS A CULTIC SUBSTITUTE FOR RELIGION SO AS TO SUSTAIN ART'S ECONOMIC VALUE AND THEIR OWN CLASS POWER.

Benjamin had fond hopes that the aura of the work of art would disappear in the wake of the advent of photography. In "The Work of Art in the Age of Mechanical Reproduction" (1936), Benjamin proclaimed:

FOR THE FIRST TIME IN WORLD HISTORY, MECHANICAL REPRODUCTION EMANCIPATES THE WORK OF ART FROM ITS PARASITICAL DEPENDENCE ON RITUAL.

Benjamin proposed that the inherent reproducibility of the photographic negative counters the auratic myth of the work of art as original and unique.

The Radical Power of Early Photographs

Benjamin's investigations into photography included an essay on its early history, "A Small History of Photography" (1931). Benjamin located a moment of radical political potential in this history. He sensed an immediacy about the first photographic portraits, despite the fact that exposures took several minutes, and that head-holders and knee-bracers were often required to maintain the sitters' pose.

Benjamin wrote passionately about these early photographic portraits, attempting to convey an experience of freedom beyond bourgeois constraints and conventions in what the photographs were unable to fix and contain. About a portrait by **David Octavius Hill** (1802–70) of a Newhaven fishwife, Benjamin wrote:

"We encounter something new and strange … her eyes cast down in such indolent, seductive modesty, there remains something that goes beyond testimony to the photographer's art, something that cannot be silenced, that fills you with an unruly desire to know what her name was, the woman who was alive there, who even now is still real and will never consent to be wholly absorbed in art."

The Fragments of History

Benjamin believed that political commitment required the writer and historian to be an **imagist**.

THE TRUE PICTURE OF THE PAST FLITS BY. THE PAST CAN BE SEIZED ONLY AS AN IMAGE WHICH FLASHES UP AT THE INSTANT WHEN IT CAN BE RECOGNIZED AND IS NEVER SEEN AGAIN.

Benjamin, himself, followed the spirit of this dictum in his massive history of the origins of modernity, "The Arcades Project" (1927–40). This project consisted entirely of quotations mined from archival sources relating to the formations of class identities in Paris under the reign of Napoleon III from 1851 to 1870. Rather than writing about the past as a complete story, in this project Benjamin undermined the ideology of an authoritative voice by flashing up images as fragments.

Theodor Adorno

Benjamin committed suicide fleeing the Nazis in 1940. However, his friend and compatriot **Theodor Adorno** (1903–69) survived the war and went on to interrogate the legacy of the Enlightenment and the part it played in the Holocaust. Like Heidegger (see pages 96–100), Adorno believed that science and technology's attempts to control and objectify nature paved the way for exploitation. In contrast to Romanticism, which attempted, through extremes of experience, to maintain a sense of individuality in the face of modern progress, Adorno asserted that the self was modernity's first victim.

THE "I" IS THE FIRST COMMODITY.

THE NAZI DEATH CAMPS AND THE MEGATON BOMB WERE A DIRECT OUTCOME OF THE ATTEMPT BY INSTRUMENTAL REASON, THROUGH TECHNOLOGY, TO DOMINATE THE SUBJECT.

Art After the Holocaust?

Following the horrific events of the Second World War, Adorno declared that there can be no real history. For Adorno, the Holocaust was so monstrous that it defies any attempt to represent or comprehend it. He believed that after this event the representation of history always seems inadequate. Art too, is rendered useless and therefore, perverse in the face of the Holocaust

TO WRITE LYRIC POETRY AFTER AUSCHWITZ IS BARBARIC.

In answer to his question, "Does art now have a right to exist; is intellectual regression not inherent in the concept of committed literature because of the regression of society?", Adorno perceived that art today is in a paradoxical situation. In his opinion, even Arnold Schönberg's composition for voice and orchestra *Survivor of Warsaw* (1947), however faithful to its violent and painful subject-matter, reduces suffering to mere images.

Adorno recognized that aesthetics – both art and theory – is one of the important battlegrounds where oppression and resistance are fought out. He refuted philosophy's totalizing tendency to provide universal theories concerning the work of art. Books such as *Negative Dialectics* (1966) and *Minima Moralia* (1951) adopted an aphoristic style in the manner of Nietzsche's writings in order to undermine philosophy's former universalizing aspirations.

Despite his customary pessimism, Adorno retained an affirmative, even utopian, sense of the potential of works of art.

EVEN IN THE MOST SUBLIMATED WORK OF ART THERE IS A HIDDEN "IT SHOULD BE OTHERWISE".

The Hollowed Subject

Like Benjamin and Brecht, Adorno criticized naturalistic art and literature. And like them, he believed that modernist art and literature possessed more suitable qualities to represent the alienation of modern life and experience under Capitalism.

IN THE LITERATURE OF FRANZ KAFKA OR SAMUEL BECKETT THE ADMINISTERED WORLD OF MONOPOLY CAPITALISM ONLY APPEARS AS BACKGROUND ---

--- YET IT EXPRESSES THE HOLLOWING OUT OF THE SUBJECT AND OF REALITY MORE FAITHFULLY AND MORE POWERFULLY THAN OTHER, SUPPOSEDLY MORE REALISTIC LITERATURE.

For Adorno, the story of Kafka's *Metamorphosis* (1915), which tells of a young man transformed into a helpless, gigantic insect, is a potent allegory of the impoverishment of experience under Capitalism.

Nietzschean Aesthetics

Martin Heidegger

As with Marx, Nietzsche's influence upon subsequent philosophy and aesthetics was profound. His ideas were espoused particularly by the German philosopher **Martin Heidegger** (1889–1976), who wrote a series of four volumes about Nietzsche between 1936 and 1946. Heidegger believed that Nietzsche's ideas represented a "twisting free of metaphysics". By this he meant that Nietzsche was the first philosopher to fully embrace art and the senses by assigning them the status of truth. In this context, Heidegger was fond of quoting Nietzsche's statement:

WE OUGHT TO BE GRATEFUL TO OUR SENSES FOR THEIR SUBTLETY, FULLNESS AND FORCE, AND WE OUGHT TO OFFER THEM IN RETURN THE VERY BEST OF SPIRIT WE POSSESS.

Nietzsche believed that aesthetic experience was grounded in the body's libido. However, Heidegger did not entirely embrace Nietzsche's physiological language, preferring an analysis of philosophy and art in terms of a concept of Being which alluded to the elusiveness of meaning and its paradoxical relevance for knowledge as well as a revised sense of place and time. For Heidegger, art had the capacity to present this paradox. Referring to Dürer's images of animals, Heidegger stated:

HE MAKES BEING ITSELF VISIBLE: IN A PARTICULAR HARE, THE BEING OF THE HARE, IN A PARTICULAR ANIMAL, THE ANIMALITY.

Although it is difficult to capture meaning – for example, the meaning of a hare – Heidegger believes that Dürer's art does convey something about the nature or Being of an animal.

The Happening of Truth

Heidegger was concerned that modernity separates us from an experience of art beyond utilitarian considerations. Like Adorno, his account of art was formulated in direct opposition to the tendency since the Enlightenment to define the truth predominantly in terms of the capacity to objectify and measure the world through science. The consequence of this, for Heidegger, was a degraded and reduced conception of technology. Heidegger believed that art was an alternative way of discovering the truth about the world and Nature.

In his essay "The Origin of the Work of Art" (1935), Heidegger turned to a painting of shoes by Van Gogh to explicate his point about art as "the happening of truth":

"A pair of peasant shoes and nothing more. And yet – From the dark opening of the worn insides of the shoes the toilsome tread of the worker stares forth … In the shoes vibrates the silent call of the earth, its quiet gift of the ripening grain and its unexplained self-refusal in the fallow desolation of the wintry field."

Heidegger's argument is that Van Gogh's painting re-creates the lived context of the peasant's life. Because the painting achieves this, Heidegger concludes:

Heidegger's reading of Van Gogh's painting is part of the tradition of **hermeneutics**, in which the work of art is seen as a clue or symptom for a wider sense of reality.

Georges Bataille

Nietzsche's vision in *The Will to Power as Art* in the 1880s of a libidinal Dionysian energy had a profound effect upon a number of Surrealist intellectuals and social scientists in the 1920s and 30s who founded the Collège de Sociologie. These included the novelist and philosopher **Georges Bataille** (1897–1962).

LIKE NIETZSCHE, I TAKE THE NOTION OF ART TO MEAN EXPERIENCE AT ITS LIMITS.

Pursuing this idea, he developed a philosophy which was fundamentally excessive and anti-utilitarian in character.

The Philosophy of Expenditure

Bataille admired the Aztecs who, he claimed, prized expenditure and loss over production and accumulation.

LUXURY, MOURNING, WAR, CULTS, THE CONSTRUCTION OF SUMPTUARY MONUMENTS, GAMES, SPECTACLES, ARTS, PERVERSE SEXUAL ACTIVITY (DEFLECTED FROM GENITAL FINALITY) REPRESENTED ACTIVITIES WHICH HAVE NO END BEYOND THEMSELVES.

Rather than being governed by an ideology of "balancing the books", in which economic and libidinal expenditure is offset by the desire for a compensatory income, as in Capitalist ideology and economics, the Aztecs believed in unconditional expenditure.

This philosophy of expenditure is the key, according to Bataille, to understanding the Aztecs' worship of the sun and their practice of human sacrifice.

MOST OF THE VICTIMS WERE PRISONERS OF WAR, JUSTIFYING THE IDEA THAT WARS WERE NECESSARY TO THE LIFE OF THE SUN: WARS HAVING THE SENSE OF CONSUMPTION, NOT THAT OF CONQUEST.

THE MEXICANS THOUGHT THAT, IF THEY CEASED, THE SUN WOULD CEASE TO BLAZE.

Bataille argued that the Aztecs conceived of the sun as a source of endless consumption and uninhibited waste. Sacrifice and war, therefore, were a means of returning energy to its solar trajectory.

The Pursuit of the Extreme

Based on his investigations into Aztec ritual and beliefs, Bataille equated desire with the pursuit of the extreme.

Such a sense of excess is exemplified by Van Gogh's "practice of staring out of the window at the blinding sphere of the sun". Van Gogh's "irrational" behaviour was motivated by a wilful urge to connect with the solar economy governing Nature.

Psychoanalysis and Aesthetics after the Second World War

Jacques Lacan

In 1945 the French psychoanalyst **Jacques Lacan** (1901–81) employed Freudian theories to analyse the formation of the sovereign Subject and the boundaries of subjective experience. In his essay "The Mirror-Phase as Formative of the Function I" (1949), Lacan suggested that the Subject's psychic roots lay in the unconscious creation of a specular, fantasized mirror image.

Lacan imagined a scenario in which an eighteen-month-old child is placed in front of a mirror by his mother. Unable to see his mother's supporting hands in the mirror, the child gains a mistaken image of himself as an independent being, capable of standing by himself.

I DESCRIBE THIS AS A FORM OF "MISRECOGNITION", AND SUGGEST THAT THE CHILD'S FANTASY OF BEING AN AUTONOMOUS SUBJECT PERSISTS INTO ADULTHOOD.

Language and the Autonomous "I"

Lacan argued that misrecognition is sustained by language. Like the specular image adopted by the young child, language creates the false assumption that the individual is autonomous and self-determining through the use of the Subject "I".

THIS "I", WHICH IS THE STARTING POINT OF GRAMMAR, IS FUNDAMENTAL TO THE CONSTRUCTION OF THE IDEOLOGY OF THE SOVEREIGN SUBJECT.

I THINK THEREFORE I AM ...

WE WON'T GET RID OF GOD UNTIL WE GET RID OF GRAMMAR.

Lacan was assisted in his critique of the Subject by his understanding of linguistic theories proposed by **Ferdinand de Saussure** (1857–1913) in his posthumously published book *A Course in General Linguistics* (1916). Saussure demonstrated that meaning does not reside in words themselves (which he termed **signifiers**), but in a potentially infinite series of differential *relationships* between signifiers.

Saussure's theory of the "arbitrary" nature of what is signified, the **sign**, became the basis for the discipline of **semiotics**: the study of signs and their variable meanings. Following the radical critiques of consciousness by Marx, Freud and Nietzsche, Saussure knocked the last nails into the coffin of the sovereign Subject.

MEANING CANNOT BE PRESENT TO ITSELF SINCE IT IS DEPENDENT UPON OTHER MEANINGS.

Following Saussure, Lacan suggested that the unconscious is like language, meaning that there is no unified Subject within the unconscious.

The Gaze

As a way of demonstrating his ideas about the limits of the Subject, Lacan referred to the construction of "the gaze" in Hans Holbein's painting of *The Ambassadors* (1533). In the right-hand side foreground of *The Ambassadors* there appears a weirdly distorted object. Seen from a high angle to the right of the painting, this object turns out to be a skull. This illusionistic device is called **anamorphosis**.

WHEN THE ILLUSION OF THE SKULL IS PERCEIVED FROM THE RIGHT OF THE PAINTING, THE IMAGE OF THE AMBASSADORS BECOMES DISTORTED AND UNGRASPABLE.

This contradiction reveals the blind-spot in the visual field of the Subject and how it is impossible to fully grasp the whole of the visual field.

The Fantasy of Control

Lacan's contemporary, the existential philosopher **Jean-Paul Sartre** (1905–80), described this blind spot in terms of anxiety. In his book *Being and Nothingness* (1943), Sartre pictured himself alone in a public park surveying the scene in front of him. Believing he has the park to himself, he is able to imagine that everything is organized from his point of view. But with the entry of another visitor to the park, Sartre's fantasy of control is violently interrupted by a feeling of not being able to grasp the whole scene for himself.

Jouissance

However, Lacan valued and affirmed the blind spot in visuality.

Lacan felt that experiences occurring in the blind spot of our knowledge and perception can be the source of a libidinal pleasure which he termed *jouissance*. According to Lacan, *jouissance* is an experience not readily accessible to language and the construction of the ego. In Lacan's terms, the scenario described by Sartre reminds the Subject of their vulnerability and engenders a pleasure in recognizing that identity is fragmented.

The eruption of experiences beyond the Subject's grasp are normally thought to lead to suffering, as in Sartre, or depression and even psychosis. Kant tried to regulate these experiences under the law of Reason. But Lacan believed that they are integral to pleasure and art precisely because they are unregulated and beyond consciousness. This is something which Lacan observed in *The Ecstasy of St Theresa* (1644–7) by **Lorenzo Bernini** (1598–1680).

YOU ONLY HAVE TO GO AND LOOK AT BERNINI'S STATUE OF ST THERESA IN ROME TO UNDERSTAND THAT SHE IS COMING.

SHE IS EXPERIENCING IT – BUT KNOWS NOTHING ABOUT IT.

Marxist Theories of the Image in the 1960s and 70s

Louis Althusser

Lacan's ideas about the formation of subjectivity and language had an impact upon Marxist intellectuals in the period around the political riots of 1968 in France. In 1970 **Louis Althusser** (1918–90) adapted Lacan's analysis of the mirror phase to his theory of ideology. Ideology, Althusser suggested, is the Subject's false sense of independence from social and economic constraints. Like Lacan, Althusser believed that ideology sprang from the assumptions generated by language concerning the autonomy of the Subject or "I".

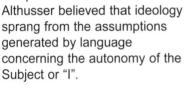

THESE ASSUMPTIONS ENGENDER THE FANTASY THAT THE SUBJECT LIVES IN A "SPONTANEOUS" AND "NATURAL" MANNER.

Debord and the Society of the Spectacle

Another Marxist intellectual influenced by Lacan's ideas was **Guy Debord** (b. 1931), who published a critique of Capitalist ideology entitled *Society of the Spectacle* (1960). With a deliberate allusion to Imperialism, Debord described Capitalism's overwhelming hold on consumerism as "the colonization of everyday life".

THE SPECTACLE IS CAPITAL ACCUMULATED UNTIL IT BECOMES AN IMAGE.

This statement referred to Capitalism's infiltration into all areas of life, including urbanism, leisure, advertising and the media.

For Debord, the "colonization of everyday life" occurs at the level of the subconscious as much as at the level of conscious experience. Conflict and class differences are airbrushed out of available information to such an extent that the Subject may simply accept this spectacle as the true state of affairs.

Lack

By definition, however, ideals are impossible to obtain. Consumerism leaves the Subject's desire unfulfilled and wanting more. Lacan described this scenario of desire and impossible fulfilment in terms of "lack". Debord believed that Capitalism exploits the experience of "lack" in order to stimulate desire and maintain the Subject in thrall to Capitalist ideals. Debord's writings mimicked Capitalism's auto-productive colonization of the unconscious in tautologies which read like soothing advertising slogans.

The Situationist International

As a member of a loosely-knit group of artists and writers known as the Situationist International, Debord formulated irrational modes of behaviour designed to obstruct Capitalist ideology. One of the Situationists' favourite methods in this regard was the *dérive* – literally meaning "drifting" – based, in part, on the 19th-century Parisian figure of the *flâneur* who blended with the city's consuming masses while maintaining an impervious distance from them.

Arising out of their interest in the *dérive*, the Situationists proposed new psycho-geographical designs based on movements of crowds. They identified the crowd's interaction with the city in terms of "constant currents, fixed points and vortexes". Based on this analysis, the Situationists planned innovative forms of mapping the city.

Détournement

In contrast to the Dadaists of the 1920s, who were self-styled
anarchists, the Situationist International wished to promote an art
form which was pointless rather than actively offensive. To this end,
the Situationists devised a strategy of *détournement* in art – the
re-use of pre-existing artistic elements in a new ensemble intended
to obviate the original sense of the elements.

FAR FROM AIMING AT AROUSING INDIGNATION OR
LAUGHTER BY ALLUDING TO SOME ORIGINAL WORK, THE
DÉTOURNED ELEMENTS EXPRESS OUR INDIFFERENCE
TOWARDS A MEANINGLESS AND FORGOTTEN ORIGINAL,
WHILE RENDERING A CERTAIN SUBLIMITY.

Ways of Seeing

Whereas Debord understood Capitalist imagery, whether in art or advertising, to play upon the spectator's sense of "lack", the British Marxist critic **John Berger** (b. 1926) believed that it operates in a more imperious manner. For Berger, this trait is exemplified by Holbein's *The Ambassadors*, the most important aspect of which is the ambassadors' sense of indifference towards the viewer.

THEY LOOK AS THOUGH THEY ARE LOOKING AT SOMETHING OF WHICH THEY ARE NOT PART.

AT THE BEST IT MAY BE A CROWD HONOURING THEM, AT THE WORST, INTRUDERS.

By emphasizing the subjugation of the viewer by the ambassadors, Berger's intention is not only to highlight the Imperialist tenor of Holbein's painting but also the continuing presence of this ideology within Capitalism.

In his book *Ways of Seeing* (1972), which was based on a television series, Berger drew analogies between genres in painting – the nude, portraiture, still life and landscape – and advertising and media images. Influenced by feminism, Berger argued that nude painting from the Renaissance onwards reflected patriarchal power in the same way as pornography.

IN BOTH OF THESE GENRES, WOMAN TURNS HERSELF INTO AN OBJECT — AND MOST PARTICULARLY AN OBJECT OF VISION: A SIGHT.

Modernist Aesthetics: 1940–70

Despite the radical critiques of the Subject proposed by the Marxist, Nietzschean and psychoanalytic traditions, Modernist ideology concerning the autonomy of experience persisted through the 1940s and 50s. Thus, the Abstract Expressionist artists in America, including **Robert Motherwell** (1915–91), **Barnett Newman** (1905–70), **Jackson Pollock** (1912–56) and **Mark Rothko** (1903–70), continued to rationalize their work as a medium of "pure" emotion.

WE ARE FREEING OURSELVES OF THE IMPEDIMENTS OF MEMORY, ASSOCIATION, NOSTALGIA, LEGEND, MYTH, OR WHAT HAVE YOU, THAT HAVE BEEN THE DEVICES OF WESTERN EUROPEAN PAINTING.

INSTEAD OF MAKING CATHEDRALS OUT OF CHRIST, MAN OR "LIFE", WE ARE MAKING IT OUT OF OURSELVES, OUT OF OUR FEELINGS.

Barnett Newman

Concurrent with Abstract Expressionism, the American art critics **Clement Greenberg** (1909–94) and his protégé **Michael Fried** (b. 1939) developed a new theory of Modernist aesthetics. Rather than stating that "pure" experience is derived from the emotions embodied in the work of art, like previous Modernist theorists, they suggested that correct judgements concerning the progressiveness of a work of art in terms of its formal properties are disinterested and pure.

MODERNIST PAINTING IS DEFINED BY AN ONGOING PROCESS OF STRESSING THE INELUCTABLE FLATNESS OF ITS SUPPORT.

BY SUPPORT, I MEAN THE PAINTING'S TWO-DIMENSIONAL SURFACE.

In somewhat elitist fashion, both Greenberg and Fried sought to preserve a form of experience – the appreciation of the formal properties of works of art – from the otherwise compromised and alienating effects of modernity and Capitalism.

Clement Greenberg

Greenberg's and Fried's ideas were derived from the aesthetic theories of the German dramatist and literary critic **Gotthold Ephraim Lessing** (1729–81). Lessing developed his theories in response to an analysis of the classical sculpture of the *Laocoon* written by his compatriot **Johann Joachim Winckelmann** (1717–68) in his *History of Ancient Art* (1764). The sculpture depicts the death of Laocoon and his sons, killed by serpents.

LAOCOON HIMSELF IS NOT SHOWN CRYING OUT IN AGONY BECAUSE THE SCULPTURE WAS INTENDED TO ILLUSTRATE GREEK STOICISM AND RESOLUTENESS.

Lessing disagreed with Winckelmann's interpretation, saying in "Laocoon, An Essay on the Limits of Poetry and Painting" (1766) that the artist understood the nature of his medium – that stone could not speak.

According to Lessing, each artistic medium possesses an innate quality which dictates what can be realized in that medium.

PAINTING CAN USE BUT A SINGLE MOMENT OF ACTION, AND MUST THEREFORE CHOOSE THE MOST PREGNANT ONE, THE ONE MOST SUGGESTIVE OF WHAT HAS GONE BEFORE AND WHAT IS TO FOLLOW.

ACTIONS ARE THE PECULIAR SUBJECTS OF POETRY AS THESE SUCCEED EACH OTHER IN TIME.

Lessing defined painting and sculpture as **spatial arts**, and poetry as a medium of **temporal succession**.

Minimalist Art

In the 1960s, both Greenberg and Fried were confounded by the Minimalist art of **Carl André** (b. 1935), **Dan Flavin** (1933–96), **Don Judd** (1928–94), **Robert Morris** (b. 1931) and **Sol Le Witt** (b. 1928), since it did not conform to the idea of sculpture as a purely spatial medium. Minimalist objects and installations were conceived in series employing multiple units and parts.

Carl André

Aesthetics, Contemporary Experience and Postmodernism

The term "postmodernism" gained currency in the 1980s both as a means of denoting a new, globalized economic order and as a way of indicating the widespread interest, particularly in Continental philosophy, in the implications of Nietzsche's philosophy and his re-evaluation of aesthetic experience.

MARXIST AND PSYCHOANALYTIC THEORIES CONTINUE TO HAVE A SIGNIFICANT BEARING UPON CONTINENTAL PHILOSOPHY ---

--- BUT THEY HAVE BEEN RETHOUGHT IN THE LIGHT OF NIETZSCHE'S IDEAS.

Gilles Deleuze

Although Marxist, psychoanalytic and Nietzschean theories were conceived at the beginning of the modern period, they continue to inform contemporary, "postmodern" aesthetics.

In Britain and America, however, where Nietzsche's influence has not been so strong, the situation has been significantly different. The American cultural historian **Fredric Jameson** (b. 1934) popularized the term postmodernism through a number of influential articles and books published in the 1980s and 90s.

IN CONTRAST TO CONTINENTAL PHILOSOPHERS, I BELIEVE THAT INDIVIDUAL AND COLLECTIVE CONSCIOUSNESS IS THE CONTINUING BATTLEGROUND OF OPPRESSION AND CLASS CONFLICT ---

--- AS WELL AS THE POTENTIAL FOR REVOLUTION AND FREEDOM.

In this respect, Jameson's theories of contemporary experience are shaped predominantly by the Marxist intellectual tradition.

The Rise of the Multinationals

According to Jameson, postmodern society is characterized by the emergence of multinational corporations. Using new forms of information technology, the exchange of Capital is dispersed across numerous networks such that it becomes almost impossible to trace exactly where power resides and how it functions. Echoing Adorno's bleak pronouncement regarding the relationship of politics and culture, where art is rendered useless by power, Jameson declared that "postmodern culture is the internal and superstructural expression of a whole new wave of American military and economic domination throughout the world".

IN THIS SENSE, AS THROUGHOUT CLASS HISTORY, THE UNDERSIDE OF CULTURE IS BLOOD, TORTURE, DEATH AND HORROR.

The complex interrelationships of economic exchange and power give rise to a sense of disorientation which Jameson sees reflected in recent architecture. John Portman's Bonaventura Hotel (1976) in downtown Los Angeles aspires to be a complete space in itself, yet entrances to the hotel are indirect and confusing, while inside the hotel's vast atrium orientation is impossible.

THE DISJUNCTION BETWEEN THE BODY AND THE BUILT ENVIRONMENT REPRESENTED BY BUILDINGS SUCH AS THE BONAVENTURA HOTEL IS AN ANALOGUE OF AN EVEN SHARPER DILEMMA ---

--- WHICH IS THE INCAPACITY OF OUR MINDS TO MAP THE GREAT GLOBAL MULTINATIONAL NETWORK IN WHICH WE FIND OURSELVES CAUGHT.

Modernist vs Postmodernist

As a way of examining the increasingly close relationship between postmodern culture and Capital, Jameson compares examples of modernist with postmodernist art and architecture. In Heidegger's interpretation of Van Gogh's peasant shoes in "The Origin of the Work of Art" (1935), the shoes were seen to stand for a wider reality. But, according to Jameson, Andy Warhol's *Diamond Dust Shoes* (1980) "no longer speaks to us with any of the immediacy of Van Gogh's footgear".

HERE WE HAVE A RANDOM COLLECTION OF DEAD OBJECTS, REMINISCENT OF THE PILE OF SHOES LEFT OVER FROM AUSCHWITZ, OR THE REMAINDERS AND TOKENS OF SOME INCOMPREHENSIBLE AND TRAGIC FIRE IN A PACKED DANCE HALL.

THERE IS NO WAY TO RESTORE TO THESE ODDMENTS A WHOLE LARGER LIVED CONTEXT.

For Jameson, even the nature of alienation and tragedy has changed in the contemporary era. In the modern period, images of alienation, such as *The Scream* (1894) by **Edvard Munch** (1863–1944), represented the breakdown of bourgeois ideals of family life and stable identity. They were, therefore, critical of bourgeois ideology. Contemporary images of alienation, however, like Warhol's series of Marilyn Monroe, are not opposed to ideology even though they possess a sense of tragedy.

RATHER, THEY REPRODUCE A SEEMINGLY ENDLESS FASCINATION WITH GLAMOUR, STARDOM AND COMMODIFICATION.

Parody or Pastiche?

Whereas modernism embraced parody as a weapon of satire opposed to bourgeois norms, postmodernism indulges in pastiche – a form of "blank irony" lacking a critical edge. Gustav Mahler's punctuation of high orchestral pathos with village accordion sentiment, or D.H. Lawrence's use of a colloquial style to pay tribute to Nature are examples of parody.

EFFECTIVELY, THESE EXAMPLES PLACE GRAND SENTIMENTS IN QUOTATION MARKS SO AS TO UNDERMINE THEM AND PREVENT THEM FROM COMING ACROSS AS OVERBLOWN AND SENTIMENTAL.

Pastiche, like parody, can be humorous but in Jameson's view it is, ultimately, imitative: a dead language.

STRAVINSKY'S ECLECTICISM AND BORROWINGS FROM OTHER COMPOSERS ANTICIPATED PASTICHE.

CONTEMPORARY ARCHITECTURE'S CANNIBALIZATION OF PAST HISTORICAL STYLES IS A FULL-BLOWN EXAMPLE OF POSTMODERN PASTICHE.

In this scenario, pastiche has no aim other than that of achieving a sense of style.

Schizophrenic Culture

Given the increasing domination of Capital and the emphasis upon surface effects, Jameson describes postmodern culture as "schizophrenic". Adapting the theories of the Swiss linguist Ferdinand de Saussure, he defines schizophrenia as an endless slippage of meaning resulting in a constant forestalling of signification. Jameson believes that this describes Capitalism's own structuring of desire which promises gratification yet defers it endlessly.

Antonio Negri and T.J. Clark

Postmodernism is sometimes equated with the development of the new technology of "information" and the internet. The cultural analyst **Antonio Negri** (b. 1933) celebrates this development.

IT OVERCOMES TRADITIONAL NOTIONS OF SPACE AND TIME AND PAVES THE WAY FOR A NEW GLOBAL COMMUNITY WITH GREATER ACCESS TO INFORMATION.

Negri claims that the creation of this virtual age implies a new primacy of the **visual** over the **verbal**, with the implication that images are easier and freer forms of communication than language.

Others are more sceptical of the claims made for these technological developments, seeing them as a thinly disguised cover for Capitalist expansion and globalization. The contemporary Marxist art historian **T.J. Clark** (b. 1943), for instance, refutes Negri's proposals, pointing out that contemporary culture, far from being emancipated by images, is in fact flooded with verbiage!

CONTEMPORARY NOTIONS OF IMAGE CLARITY, IMAGE FLOW AND DENSITY ARE ALL MODELLED ON THE PARALLEL AND UNIMPEDED MOVEMENTS OF THE LOGO, THE COMPRESSED PSEUDONARRATIVE OF THE TV COMMERCIAL, THE PRODUCT SLOGAN, THE SOUNDBITE.

IMAGES ARE STILL EVERYWHERE TELLING STORIES OR ISSUING ORDERS.

WEB PAGES, BILLBOARDS AND VIDEO GAMES ARE JUST VISUALIZATIONS OF THE SHOUTED — OR WHISPERED — SENTENCE.

Clark points out that the ideology of mobility and the free play of appearances arose towards the end of the 19th century with the expansion of the bourgeoisie and the beginning of a consumer society.

In Clark's view, contemporary global society is still under the sway of Capitalist ideologies stemming from the beginning of the modern era.

Postmodernism and Continental Aesthetics

Jean Baudrillard

Perhaps the closest of contemporary French philosophers to Fredric Jameson's position is **Jean Baudrillard** (b. 1929). As with Jameson, Baudrillard's work is influenced by Marx, but his writing is more nihilistic and ironic than Jameson's. Following Debord, Baudrillard recognized that the motor of Capital is the consumer's desire, rather than the alienation of labour as Marx maintained.

CAPITAL OPERATES IN TERMS OF THE SAME IDEOLOGY AS IN SAUSSURE'S ANALYSIS OF LANGUAGE ...

CONSUMERISM IS A POTENTIALLY INFINITE PROCESS OF NEVER SATIATED DESIRE.

THE VALUE OF COMMODITIES, LIKE THE MEANING OF WORDS, IS SUBJECT TO AN ENDLESS PROCESS OF REDEFINITION WHICH, ULTIMATELY, NO ONE CONTROLS.

The Medium is the Message

Baudrillard agreed with Marshall McLuhan's famous dictum, "the medium is the message". Capitalism, for Baudrillard, is an arena of mutually reinforcing, self-referential images and signs.

TAKE A TYPICAL EXAMPLE: IN WINTER ESSO SELLS FIREWOOD AND BARBECUE KITS AT ITS SERVICE STATIONS.

HERE ARE THE CHAMPIONS OF PETROL, THE "HISTORICAL LIQUIDATORS" OF FIREWOOD AND ITS WHOLE SYMBOLIC VALUE, WHO SERVE IT UP TO YOU AGAIN AS THE NEO-FIREWOOD ESSO.

"Reality" is beyond representation: what "the masses" really think or want remains in the realm of fantasy, the product of an accumulation of information and opinion polls!

The Aesthetics of Simulation

Baudrillard defined Capitalism as "the exaltation of signs based on the denial of the reality of things". This situation, Baudrillard claimed, engenders a different form of aesthetics from previously: an aesthetics of **simulation** rather than an aesthetics of beauty and originality. In Baudrillard's opinion, the world is made up of copies of other copies: a fact exemplified by Pop art in the 1960s.

POP IS AT ONE WITH INDUSTRIAL AND SERIAL PRODUCTION, AND THUS WITH THE ARTIFICIAL OR MANUFACTURED CHARACTER OF THE WHOLE ENVIRONMENT.

Baudrillard contrasted the "cool" art of Pop with the "hot" painting of Abstract Expressionism which was seen as a radical gesture of independence from cultural constraints and laws.

BUT ABSTRACT EXPRESSIONISM IS NO MORE RADICAL OR "REAL" THAN POP.

IT CONFRONTS A FULL, SATURATED SYSTEM OF SIGNS WITH A PURE AND EMPTY GESTURE, WHICH CELEBRATES ITS OWN DISAPPEARANCE.

At its most extreme, Abstract Expressionism is nihilistic and akin to an act of terrorism, with little real power to effect change. Ultimately, Abstract Expressionism is no more than an explosive dream.

The Ironies of Postmodern Capitalism

As his work developed, Baudrillard's writings became more aphoristic, concerned with the ironies of postmodern Capitalism. Baudrillard is particularly ironic about the differences between postmodern society as a culture of simulation and ancient societies of the sacred, as described by Bataille (about which Baudrillard is under no illusions, describing Aztec culture as "the universe of cruelty").

SNOW IS NO LONGER A GIFT FROM ON HIGH. IT FALLS PRECISELY AT THOSE PLACES DESIGNATED AS WINTER RESORTS.

A recurring theme of postmodern aesthetics in the Continental mode is the idea that experience no longer exists in a pure state, autonomous from language, as Kant posited. Instead, experience exists at the limits of language and identity where the edges begin to blur. Following Nietzsche, experience is envisaged as an emotional excess escaping the Subject's grasp.

Roland Barthes

One of the most influential of postmodern philosophers on the
Continent is **Roland Barthes** (1915–80), whose work became
increasingly concerned with experience at the borders of language.
Prior to the 1960s, Barthes applied Saussure's linguistic theories
(see page 107) to a variety of cultural forms and artefacts.
Mythologies (1957), a collection of short essays, analysed the
semiology (the meaning of signs and symbols) in popular culture
and how historical and moral references are encoded. The essays
included a study of the way in which hair fringes connote
"Roman-ness" in a Hollywood film of *Julius Caesar*, an analysis
of wrestling as a theatrical mime concerned with Justice …

Messages Without a Code

In the early 1960s, Barthes began to concentrate upon an experience of film and photography which exceeds language and semiological connotation – the culturally formed meanings of signs and symbols. Using an advertisement for Panzani pasta products as an example, Barthes maintained that, despite its use of connotation to signify "Italianicity" (green, red and white colours, plum tomatoes and spaghetti), it possessed another level without connotation derived from the fact that the photographic negative is an authentic trace of reality, made by light travelling between the subject of the photograph and the sensitized film. This direct link remains in a pure form, whatever meanings are constructed around it.

The Punctum

In his final book, *Camera Lucida* (1980), Barthes developed a notion of "the punctum", an effect of being moved and rendered speechless by the photographic image. The punctum effect arises out of Barthes' astonishment that the people he is looking at – who seem so vivid and alive – have grown older or have even died.

Camera Lucida revolves around the discussion of a photograph of Barthes' mother as a child, which is deliberately not reproduced in the book. In this photograph Barthes discovers a vision of the essence of his late mother's gentleness and generosity which defies even death. The photograph transports Barthes to another time when his mother was alive, and leads him to ruminate upon the contradictions of time in photography.

IN A PHOTOGRAPH THE PERSON DEPICTED SEEMS TO HAVE AN EXTENDED LIFE (EVEN THOUGH HE OR SHE IS NO LONGER THE SAME) ---

--- WHILE THE VIEWER BECOMES AWARE OF THEIR OWN MORTALITY IN BEHOLDING THE EXTENDED LIFE OF THE SUBJECT IN THE PHOTOGRAPH.

Influenced by both Barthes and Lacan, the work of **Julia Kristeva** (b. 1941) has consistently explored the idea of experience as a form of loss. She argues that certain forms of literature and art reveal a level to the unconscious which exceeds patriarchy's conception of identity.

In books such as *Desire in Language* (1977), *Powers of Horror* (1980) and *Black Sun: Depression and Melancholia* (1987), Kristeva provides an important "feminist" understanding of identity which makes use of the post-Kantian tradition of aesthetics to conceive of pleasure as a corollary to the breakdown of coherence and sense.

Kristeva believes that certain forms of literature and art relate to early infant experiences both in the womb and after, prior to the child's acquisition of language. In this respect, Kristeva's views about art differ from Freud's. Freud believed that art is an expression of yearning and conflict stemming from the child's separation from the Mother owing to the law of the Father.

MY VIEW OF ART IS THAT IT ARISES FROM THE CHILD'S RELATIONSHIP TO THE MOTHER PRECEDING THE INTERVENTION OF THE LAW OF THE FATHER AND THE DICTATES OF SOCIETY.

According to Kristeva, an idea of what this formative space of experience is like is given by Plato in his dialogue *Timaeus* (c. 360 C), in which he mentions the idea of a "chora".

PLATO'S CHORA EVOKES A MATERNAL RECEPTACLE, A CRUSHING, DANCING RECEPTACLE.

THE GREEK WORD REFERS TO BOTH THE WOMB AND A POPULAR DANCE PERFORMED IN THE OPEN SQUARES OF THE CITY.

This chora is what Kristeva refers to as the "semiotic". The semiotic is a space of dissolution and fragmentation existing prior to language, but it is also a source of emotive experience and instinctual drives

For Kristeva, the writings of modern authors such as **Louis-Ferdinand Céline** (1894–1961), **Samuel Beckett** (1906–89), **Antonin Artaud** (1895–1948) and **James Joyce** (1882–1941) convey a sense of the semiotic.

Joyce's novels *Ulysses* (1922) and *Finnegans Wake* (1939) function on the edges of sense, testifying in a language that is "always already old, always already out of date, as funny as it is ephemeral" to the ecstatic subversion of paternal authority.

Kristeva and *Jouissance*

In the visual arts, the fresco cycles of **Giotto** (1267–1337) at Padua (c. 1304) and Assisi (c. 1305–6) exemplify Kristeva's notion of the semiotic. The overlapping, fragmented blocks of the frescoes' scenery (fields, landscape, architecture) create "an antagonistic space".

To characterize Giotto's overthrow of geometry and paternal authority through colour and rhythm, Kristeva adopts the term *jouissance* from Lacan and Barthes, meaning (variously) joy, ecstasy, orgasm.

In *Black Sun*, Kristeva explores another side to *jouissance*, as a profound sense of melancholy and depression which she encounters in writers such as **Fyodor Dostoyevsky** (1821–81) and **Marguerite Duras** (1914–96), and in the 16th-century artist Hans Holbein.

Lacking any sense of Christian redemption, Holbein's painting *The Body of the Dead Christ in the Tomb* (1522) is utterly austere and sombre.

THE PAINTING IS NOT EVEN A REPRESENTATION AS SUCH, MORE A BLANK OR DISCONTINUITY IN REPRESENTATION.

Kristeva believes that the discontinuity exemplified by Holbein's painting is derived from the unconscious, where language and sense are overwhelmed by a profound sorrow originating from the child's conflicts with, and separation from, the Mother.

Feminist Aesthetics and Postmodernism

Kristeva's critique of patriarchy is shared by other philosophers of her generation, such as **Hélène Cixous** (b. 1937) and **Luce Irigaray** (b. 1932). In essays such as "Women on the Market" (1978), Irigaray stresses the fact that Women's oppression relies upon patriarchy's organization of identity under the sign of the phallus.

THIS SIGN IS INSCRIBED UPON WOMAN'S BODY AS A LACK (SHE "LACKS" A PENIS), WITH ALL OF THE PEJORATIVE CONNOTATIONS THAT THIS JUDGEMENT CARRIES.

Such a binary conception of identity results from an inability to conceive of difference as absolutely Other and unrepresentable, as proposed by Nietzsche.

Jacques Derrida

Like Kristeva, Cixous and Irigaray, **Jacques Derrida** (1930–2004) is also inspired by Nietzsche's approach to alterity. Recognizing the fundamental link between patriarchy and the tradition of philosophy derived from Plato's metaphysics, Derrida refers to this tradition as "phallo-logocentric", meaning that it revolves around the notion of the phallus.

Examples include:

ALL PHILOSOPHICAL CONCEPTUALIZATIONS UNTIL NIETZSCHE ARE DIVIDED INTO A FOUNDATIONAL CONCEPT (THE PHALLUS) AND A SUPPLEMENTARY CONCEPT WHICH DEPENDS UPON, BUT ALSO DEFINES, THE FORMER CONCEPT.

beauty / ugliness

truth / falsity

good / evil

masculinity / femininity

subject / other

inside / outside

Deconstruction

MY PURPOSE IS TO "DECONSTRUCT" THESE BINARY TERMS, REVEALING THEIR DEPENDENCE UPON EACH OTHER.

MY PHILOSOPHY AIMS TO PLUNGE MEANING AND TRUTH INTO QUESTION BY MARKING A THIRD, AMBIGUOUS TERM UPON WHICH BINARY OPPOSITIONS ARE STRUCTURED.

inside outside good evil

The idea of a third term appears in Derrida's book *The Truth in Painting* (1978), in which he deconstructs passages from Kant's *Critique of Judgement* and Heidegger's essay "The Origin of the Work of Art". Derrida's deconstructive work involves close readings of philosophical texts by, among others, Plato, Nietzsche, Marx, Freud and Saussure.

Discussing Kant's *Critique of Judgement*, Derrida draws attention to a passage in which Kant excludes what he considers as peripheral to aesthetic consideration: the gilded frames of paintings, the drapery on statues and the colonnades of palaces. To describe their status, Kant revives the Greek term *parergon*, meaning an adjunct to the complete representation.

So what is outside the work of art is also within it. The *parergon* is neither inside the work of art, nor outside it, but both of these things.

Undecidable Art

According to Derrida, all attempts to decipher the work of art and assign it a "truth" are driven by a proprietorial urge. By way of illustrating this point, Derrida refers to the contrasting interpretations given by Martin Heidegger (in 1935–6) and Meyer Schapiro (in 1968) of Van Gogh's *Old Shoes* (1886–7).

I IDENTIFIED THE BOOTS IN THE PAINTING AS A PAIR OF PEASANT WOMEN'S SHOES ---

--- WHEREAS I CLAIMED THAT THEY WERE THE ARTIST'S OWN SHOES AND THAT THE PAINTING IS A FORM OF SELF-PORTRAITURE.

By attempting to establish the identity of the owner of Van Gogh's shoes, both writers attempted to make sense of the painting, whereas Derrida prefers to highlight the essentially ambiguous and **undecidable** nature of the work of art's meaning and origin.

Jean-François Lyotard

Like Derrida, **Jean-François Lyotard** (1924–98) also affirmed uncertainty and doubt, stating that doubt is integral to thought: "It is only at the price of doubt that reason reasons." Lyotard argued that to be truly human we need to recover the "inhuman" in ourselves by experiencing, as in the initial stage of the sublime, a loss of control. He illustrated this idea with the example of a small child.

SHORN OF SPEECH, INCAPABLE OF STANDING UPRIGHT, HESITATING OVER THE OBJECTS OF ITS INTEREST ---

--- NOT ABLE TO CALCULATE ITS ADVANTAGES, NOT SENSITIVE TO HUMAN REASON, THE CHILD IS EMINENTLY THE HUMAN BECAUSE ITS DISTRESS HERALDS AND PROMISES THINGS POSSIBLE.

Newman and Duchamp

Lyotard upheld the notion of postmodernism as a way of describing a growing sense of alterity within contemporary culture and society. He explained this theory with reference to Barnett Newman's zip paintings, which he contrasted with *The Bride Stripped Bare By Her Bachelors, Even* (*The Large Glass*) (1915–23) and *Etant Donnés* (*Given …*) (1946–66) by **Marcel Duchamp** (1887–1968).

The Large Glass

DUCHAMP'S WORKS CAN ONLY REPRESENT TIME AS OCCURRING EITHER PRIOR TO, OR AFTER, THE EVENT.

This "event" in Duchamp's art is the recognition of sexual difference. In *The Large Glass*, the bachelors, depicted as spindles in the lower region, ejaculate over the bride in the upper area (representing time occurring prior to the event) …

Etant Donnés

… while the young woman in *Etant Donnés* submits to the traumatic recognition of her sex (representing time occurring after the event).

In contrast with Duchamp, Barnett Newman's paintings do not operate in terms of opposites. As well as being able to represent "the event", they are both **representations** and **presentations** simultaneously.

IN THE STATIONS OF THE CROSS (1958–66), THE TIME OF WHAT IS RECOUNTED (THE FLASH OF THE KNIFE RAISED AGAINST ISAAC) AND THE TIME TAKEN TO RECOUNT THAT TIME (THE CORRESPONDING VERSES OF GENESIS) ARE CONDENSED.

The abstract line of the zip *represents* time – the time of creation itself, when the open void becomes form. But it also *is* this time – the instant of creation. Together, these elements constitute "the event".

In Lyotard's opinion, Duchamp's readymades (such as *Bottle Dryer* (1914) and *Fountain* (1917)) – as opposed to works like *The Large Glass* and *Etant Donnés* – function in a similar manner to Newman's paintings as both presentations and representations. They are utilitarian objects beyond the conventional boundaries of art and art objects at the same time.

THE READYMADES EXEMPLIFY THE CONSTANT PROCESS OF DISPOSSESSION THAT THE ARTIST EXPERIENCES EVEN FROM HIS OR HER OWN WORK.

With this in mind, Lyotard agrees with the art historian Thierry de Duve that "the contemporary aesthetic question is not 'What is beautiful?' but 'What can be said to be art?'"

Lyotard stressed the fact that postmodernism is a re-evaluation of the Enlightenment and modernism, rather than an alternative to it.

MANY OF THE PREOCCUPATIONS OF MODERNISM PERSIST IN POSTMODERNISM BUT WITHOUT ITS SPIRITUAL OR PURIST TENDENCIES.

This is exemplified not just by Lyotard's philosophy, but also by that of **Gilles Deleuze** (1925–95), whose thinking is similarly influenced by Nietzsche's re-evaluation of Kant's aesthetics.

Gilles Deleuze

Like many Modernists, Deleuze claims that painting is capable of acting directly upon the nervous system: "With painting, hysteria becomes art". But, as the notion of hysteria suggests, Deleuze does not use this theory to maintain a controlling Subject within the sphere of experience, as in early Modernist aesthetics.

EXPERIENCE IS EXCESSIVE AND CONFUSED.

AS SUCH, VISUALITY IS NOT CONFINED SIMPLY TO THE EYE.

PAINTING GIVES US EYES ALL OVER: IN THE EAR, IN THE STOMACH, IN THE LUNGS (THE PAINTING BREATHES ---).

The Body without Organs

Deleuze's revised sense of visuality challenges the primacy normally given to the eye in modern aesthetics up to and including Lacan, and is part of his philosophical conception of "the body without organs". Deleuze adopted this term from the playwright **Antonin Artaud** (1895–1948), the innovator of the "Theatre of Cruelty". Deleuze's claims for the paintings of Francis Bacon as being composed of *intensities* of experience are influenced by Artaud's ideas of "the body's escape from the mind".

PAINTING IS LODGED WHERE THE BODY ESCAPES ITSELF. BUT IN ESCAPING, THE BODY DISCOVERS THE MATERIALITY OF WHICH IT IS COMPOSED.

Deleuze defined painting in psychopathological terms as a form of hysteria, whereas music's pathology is "more of a galloping schizophrenia" that speaks of disembodiment and dematerialization.

Thus, like Lessing, and like Modernists such as Greenberg and Fried, Deleuze maintains that there is an essence to different art forms, but in a way which posits the body as a conduit of psychic conflicts and experiences.

Conclusion

So at the start of the 21st century we find an aesthetics of disembodiment and fragmentation. Aesthetics has been central to the re-evaluation of the Subject since its inception by Baumgarten and Kant in the 18th century.

When Keats wrote "Ode on a Grecian Urn" in 1820 there was already a crisis in the conception of the Subject as a unified and homogeneous unit. The figures on the urn in Keats' poem are frozen in time as if they are immortal. But the poet recognized that this scene bore no relation to life or mortality.

In the poem, the Subject is fallible and mortal and, as such, beauty and truth exist beyond the Subject's grasp.

And yet, notions of beauty and truth persist in postmodernism, and not necessarily in the melancholic way that Keats conceived of them. In *The Will to Power as Art*, Nietzsche expressed another view, that beauty is not just **passive** but **transformative**.

"BEAUTY" EXISTS OUTSIDE ALL ORDERS OF RANK, BECAUSE IN BEAUTY OPPOSITES ARE TAMED.

In sum, beauty is the recognition that concepts which have traditionally been thought of as "negative" – such as failure, destruction or "lack" – are not simply negative, but also intrinsic to art, creativity and life-affirming values. Following Nietzsche, beauty has become one of the stakes involved in the re-evaluation of metaphysics, while "truth" is the realization and practice of such a philosophy.

Further Reading

As the term "aesthetics" suggests notions of experience, it relates to a wide range of ideas covered by philosophy. For the purposes of further reading, the selected texts listed here cover the relevant philosophical issues, often making particular reference to art. These texts provide a route through the multi-faceted subject of aesthetics while also being fascinating for their views and interpretations of art. Secondary reading can be supplemented with books in the Icon series introducing philosophers and the history of ideas and philosophy.

Primary texts

Theodor Adorno and Max Horkheimer, *Dialectic of Enlightenment*, New York, Seabury Press, 1972

Theodor Adorno, Walter Benjamin, Ernst Bloch, Bertolt Brecht, Georg Lukács, *Aesthetics and Politics: The Key Texts of the Classic Debate Within German Marxism*, Verso, 1986

Louis Althusser, *Essays on Ideology*, Verso, 1984

Thomas Aquinas, *The Pocket Aquinas*, ed. V. Bourke, Washington Square Press, 1969

Aristotle, *Poetics*, Penguin, 1996

Saint Augustine, *The Confessions*, Everyman Library, 2001

Roland Barthes, *Camera Lucida; Reflections on Photography* (1980), Vintage, 1993

Georges Bataille, *Visions of Excess: Selected Writings, 1927–1939*, University of Minnesota Press, 1991

Jean Baudrillard, *The Conspiracy of Art: Manifestos, Interviews, Essays*, Semiotext(e), 2005

Walter Benjamin, *Illuminations*, FontanaCollins, 1982; *One-Way Street and Other Writings*, Verso, 1992

John Berger, *Ways of Seeing*, BBC and Penguin, 1987

T.J. Clark, *Modernism, Postmodernism and Steam*, *October*, 100, Spring 2002, pp. 154–74

Guy Debord, *Society of the Spectacle*, Rebel Press, Aim Publications, 1987

Gilles Deleuze, *Nietzsche and Philosophy*, Athlone Press, 1983; *Francis Bacon: The Logic of Sensation*, Continuum, 2003

Jacques Derrida, *The Truth in Painting*, University of Chicago Press, 1987

Michel Foucault, *The Order of Things: An Archaeology of the Human*

Sciences, Tavistock Publications, 1986; *This Is Not A Pipe*, University of California Press, 1983

Sigmund Freud, *Case Histories*, vols 8 and 9; *Art and Literature*, vol. 14, Penguin Freud Library, 1990 (also published in the *Standard Edition of Freud's Psychological Works*, ed. James Strachey)

Georg Hegel, *Introductory Lectures on Aesthetics* (1820–29), Penguin, 2004

Martin Heidegger, *Being and Time*, Blackwell, 2006; *Basic Writings*, Routledge, 2004

Fredric Jameson, *Postmodernism, or the Cultural Logic of Late Capitalism*, Verso, 1991

Immanuel Kant, *Critique of Judgement* (1790), Hackett, 1987

Julia Kristeva, *Desire in Language: A Semiotic Approach to Literature and Art*, Blackwell, 1987; *Black Sun: Depression and Melancholia*, Columbia University Press, 1989

Jacques Lacan, *Écrits*, W.W. Norton, 2006; *The Four Fundamental Concepts of Psychoanalysis*, Penguin, 1991

Jean-François Lyotard, *The Postmodern Condition: A Report on Knowledge*, Manchester University Press, 1986; *The Inhuman: Reflections on Time*, Polity Press, 1993

Karl Marx, *Grundrisse*, Penguin, 2005; *Capital: A Critique of Political Economy*, vol. 1 (1867), Penguin, 1990

Friedrich Nietzsche, *Twilight of the Idols* (1888) in *The Portable Nietzsche*, Penguin, 1976; *The Will to Power* (1883–8), Vintage, 1968

Plato, *The Portable Plato*, Penguin, 1977; *Sophist*, Hackett, 1993

Jean-Paul Sartre, *Being and Nothingness: An Essay on Phenomenological Ontology*, Routledge, 2001

Ferdinand de Saussure, *Course in General Linguistics*, Duckworth, 1983

Oscar Wilde, *The Picture of Dorian Gray*, Oxford University Press, 1988

Secondary texts

Moshe Barasch, *Theories of Art* (3 vols: *From Plato to Winckelmann*, *From Winckelmann to Baudelaire*, *From Impressionism to Kandinsky*), Routledge, 2000

Andrew Bowie, *Aesthetics and Subjectivity: From Kant to Nietzsche*, Manchester University Press, 2003

Jay Bernstein (ed.), *Classic and Romantic German Aesthetics*, Cambridge University Press, 2003

David Cooper (ed.), *A Companion to Aesthetics*, Blackwell, 2003

Terry Eagleton, *The Ideology of the Aesthetic*, Blackwell, 1990

Umberto Eco (ed.), *On Beauty: A History of a Western Idea*, Secker and Warburg, 2004

Jae Emerling, *Theory For Art History*, Routledge, 2005

Berys Gaut and Dominic McIver Lopes, *The Routledge Companion to Aesthetics*, Routledge, 2002

Stephen Halliwell, *The Aesthetics of Mimesis: Ancient Texts and Modern Problems*, Princeton University Press, 2002

Charles Harrison and Paul Wood (eds), *Art in Theory, 1900–1990: An Anthology of Changing Ideas*, Blackwell, 1992

Charles Harrison, Paul Wood and Jason Gaiger (eds), *Art in Theory, 1648–1815: An Anthology of Changing Ideas*, Blackwell, 2000

Richard Kearney and David Rasmussen, *Continental Aesthetics, Romanticism to Postmodernism: An Anthology*, Blackwell, 2001

Christopher Kul-Want, *Philosophers on Art, From Kant to Postmodernism, A Reader*, Columbia University Press, forthcoming

Leonardo da Vinci, *Leonardo on Painting: An Anthology of Writings by Leonardo da Vinci*, ed. M. Kemp, Yale University Press, 1989

Author's Acknowledgements

I would like to thank Richard Appignanesi for commissioning this book, and Duncan Heath for his editing. I would also like to thank Meg Errington and Clive Hodgson for the encouragement they have given me during the writing of this book. I am particularly grateful for the advice and input I've received from my wife, Catherine Yass. This book is dedicated to her.

Christopher Kul-Want is Course Director of the MA in Fine Art at Byam Shaw School of Art, Central St Martins, University of the Arts, London. He is the author of *Introducing Kant* (Icon Books, 1996), and he is currently editing an anthology entitled *Philosophers on Art, From Kant to Postmodernism, A Reader* (Columbia University Press).

Artist's Acknowledgements

I would like to thank the people at Icon, especially Duncan. I dedicate this book to my old man and Silvina.

Piero is an illustrator and animator. He has also illustrated *Introducing Shakespeare*, *Introducing Anthropology*, *Introducing Psychiatry*, *Introducing Barthes* and *Introducing Nietzsche*. He is currently working on a comic book. **www.pieroillustration.com**

Index